VIRGINIA
CIDER

VIRGINIA CIDER

A SCRUMPTIOUS HISTORY

Alistair Reece & J. Mark Stewart

AMERICAN PALATE

Published by American Palate
A Division of The History Press
Charleston, SC
www.historypress.com

Text copyright © 2024 by Alistair Reece
Images copyright © 2024 by J. Mark Stewart

First published 2024

Manufactured in the United States

ISBN 9781467155670

Library of Congress Control Number: 9781467155670

Notice: The information in this book is true and complete to the best of our knowledge. It is offered without guarantee on the part of the author or The History Press. The author and The History Press disclaim all liability in connection with the use of this book.

For Ashley

CONTENTS

FOREWORD

Cider is Virginia's—and the United States'—oldest libation but is also the newest. The definition of cider, the beverage that everyone drank from European settlement into the nineteenth century, has had a tortuous path in this country. Cider is the fermented juice of the apple. Only in this country did the term become attributed to fresh juice, while the name for proper cider defaulted to "hard cider." In England and other parts of Europe, whence our first settlers hailed, this was not the case. Alistair Reece, originally from the United Kingdom, settled in Virginia some fifteen years ago and is well suited to explore the state's young and growing modern cider scene. Familiar with cider from his early years, he has worked extensively in craft beverages both in Europe and in this country. He brings a broad perspective and enthusiasm for local foodways that informs his examination of cider in Virginia.

Alistair's move to Virginia coincided with the opening of Albemarle CiderWorks in central Virginia. My family had begun planting apples in the early 1990s, primarily as a hobby devoted to discovering and preserving apples not commonly found in the mass distribution food emporiums served by the industrial agriculture that emerged in the twentieth century. We sought out apples with complex, interesting flavors and collected some 250 varieties, most of them heirloom varieties once widely grown but increasingly hard to find, apples that are tart, sweet, spicy, complex, vinous and on and on. These qualities are not exclusively the property of older varieties. So we named our venture Vintage Virginia Apples, *vintage* being a term that is not age-related. Our friend Tom Burford was our inspiration and guide, and we lost a great folk artist when he died in 2020. He was an indefatigable proponent and promoter of apples and, as the scion of a long line of orchardists in Amherst County, was well suited to be a modern apostle of local and heritage foodways.

Realizing that so many of the apples we were collecting had been grown for cider or had come out of the vast seedling orchards settlers had planted, primarily for cider, we founded Albemarle CiderWorks in 2007. When we opened our tasting room in 2009, we were but dimly aware that we were on the threshold of a new chapter in this country's libation and culinary experience. We are now Virginia's oldest producing modern cidery. Cider in the United States and Virginia today is crafting its identity. At Albemarle CiderWorks, we are dedicated to making fine ciders that demonstrate and promote the virtues of translating the orchard to the glass. To that end, we have enjoyed collaborating with and promoting our colleagues in the industry by precept and by example. Promoting and sustaining our vibrant orchard industry is just as important, and we are dedicated to not only growing our own apples but also encouraging our orchardists to grow varieties that translate to the glass effectively. As our public becomes more aware of what proper cider really is and discovers, as a colleague once observed, that wine is only cider made from grapes, cider will grow in acceptance and popularity, we believe.

Much of what has been written on cider in the United States today deals largely with broader regions—the Northeast, the Northwest—and perhaps rightly so, since these regions produce rather large quantities of apples and cider. Yet Virginia's production of these commodities is not insignificant, and it is growing. Educating our public is hugely important. This survey of Virginia cider makes an important contribution to that need. Alistair reviews cider's Virginian history, then moves on to an examination of the industry today. His discussion of some of the ciders available on the market illustrates and highlights what is still a somewhat rare and often misunderstood drink. By pointing out the broad diversity of styles being produced here, this work will encourage the enlightenment our public needs to appreciate fine ciders.

Charlotte Shelton
Albemarle CiderWorks, June 2024

ACKNOWLEDGEMENTS

I want to take a few lines to thank the various people, both here in Virginia and around the world, who have been invaluable to me as I have written this book.

First and foremost, thank you to my wife and twin sons, who have dealt with my disappearing away for days and weekends, driving the highways and byways of Virginia to visit, meet with and get to know so many of the cider makers mentioned in this book. To my wife in particular: thank you for your patience and forbearance as I have then hidden away in my office writing long after you have gone to bed, though I am sure you have enjoyed many of the pressed and fermented fruits of my labors.

To my longtime collaborator and amazing photographer, Mark: who would have thought that meeting in the pubs of Prague while our wives stitched and bitched would eventually lead to us creating this book? It is an honor to count you as my friend, and I look forward to more trips along the foodways and boozeways of Virginia in search of stories to tell.

In the world of publishing, I also want to thank Matt Curtis of *Pellicle* magazine in the United Kingdom, the first editor to commission writing from me. Your guidance in writing for publication has been vital and gratefully received, and you gave me the confidence to believe that my writing was actually good enough to be published in the first place. Also, thank you to my friend, and neighbor, Michael Levatino for sharing wise counsel and trade knowledge as I prepared my pitch for a book about cider in Virginia.

Ultimately this book is about the cider makers of Virginia, and so special heartfelt thanks goes out to them for embracing this project and finding time for Mark and I to visit, chat with them, ask questions and feel ourselves a part of this delightfully eclectic community. In particular, I want to give shout-outs to the Sheltons of Albemarle CiderWorks: you are the epitome of all that is great about Virginian cider, generous with your knowledge, passionate about the craft and just all-around good people. To Will and Cornelia at Troddenvale, thank you for making ciders that are, as I said at the tasting room way back when, "revelatory"; my Dolgo tree stands as a constant reminder of that trip. Every other cider maker I have spoken to for this book has likewise been an inspiration and a source of challenge (that's a good thing; I love being challenged), and your love of cider has been evident in every conversation we have had. I look forward to enjoying glasses of cider with you all again soon.

Last, but in no way least, to The History Press and Kate Jenkins specifically: thank you for seeing the value in a book about cider in Virginia as it touches the past, the present and the future and for taking a punt on a first-time author. Your support and encouragement have been superb.

Mark the photographer here, and I want to give heartfelt and hearty appreciation to my wife, Joanna, and to my two sons, for their encouragement to keep picking up that camera and exploring the far-flung regions of Virginia in search of "just the right photo" to tell the story of cider. Thanks also to the animals at Epworth Farm, who managed to avoid crises, having babies or getting their dang heads stuck in the fence while I was away from home.

And I want to thank Alistair Reece, who served as my travel companion, trip organizer and faithful conversation partner through the many hours it took to visit each of the beautiful locations that appear in this book. Alistair's research could have happened exclusively by phone interview—but he was willing to invest in the photography as much as I did, and the results do show! (Thanks to Alistair's family, as well, who gave him up on their treasured weekends so he could go apple-traipsing with me!)

Thanks to Kate Jenkins and the team at The History Press, who guided us faithfully through the publication process and who are helping bring to light the history and stories of ciders throughout the commonwealth.

And finally, thanks to the amazing community of orchard growers, apple pickers and cider makers who let me behind the counter and through the orchards as I collected the pictures that help bring this story to life. Their produce is the star of this book, and you can taste in it the energy, the creativity, the time and the struggle that is required to turn sunshine and earth into that amazingly effervescent nectar that fills our glasses and lightens our hearts.

INTRODUCTION

When three English ships sailed on from their initial landing at what is today Fort Monroe in Hampton, Virginia, they carried within their bowels the roots of far more than they ever imagined. From those beginnings came not just the settlement they named in honor of their king, Jamestown, but also the commonwealth of Virginia, as well as the genesis of both the United States of America and, eventually, even the British Empire. The 104 settlers aboard the *Susan Constant*, *Godspeed* and *Discovery* also brought with them many of the traditional English passions: a love for beef, for beer and also for cider.

Cider making in the lands that we now call England can be traced back to before the Roman conquest of Britain. On visiting the British Isles in 55 BCE, Julius Caesar found that the native Britons fermented local crab apples to make a rudimentary cider. When, eventually, the Romans invaded some one hundred years later, they brought with them many agricultural innovations that would revolutionize both fruit growing and, hence, cider making in the new Roman province of Britannia, most notably how to graft scion wood from a particularly favored tree to a rootstock so that the tree could be further propagated. While the old saying is that "the apple doesn't fall far from the tree," the truth is that the seed of that apple does not grow true to the tree from which it fell. Therefore, if you want to grow more apples just like the ones you get from that tree in your backyard that has no known varietal name, grafting is the only way to do so.

Eventually the Romans would leave, to be replaced, at least at the aristocratic level, by invaders from just over the North Sea. The Anglo-Saxons came from the modern Netherlands, Germany and southern Denmark, and within a few generations, they had adopted many of the ways and habits of the native Britons. Christianity would become the dominant religion of the British Isles. When the king of Northumbria adopted the Roman version of Christianity in 664 CE at the Synod of Whitby, there would follow a flowering of monasticism, and the monks were required to be self-sufficient, so they planted more orchards. More orchards, of course, would mean more cider.

The third invasion of England that would impact cider occurred in 1066 CE, when William of Normandy laid claim to the English throne. The Normans were also lovers of cider—as they continue to be famed for to this day—and so they brought with them French apple varieties to their newly conquered territory, adding them to the mix that, over the next five and a half centuries, would become the cider culture so beloved of the English colonists who eventually landed in the Chesapeake and established Jamestown, including an ancestor of at least one modern cider maker in Virginia.

Cider has, likewise, long been part of my life. Some of my earliest memories of summer afternoon grill outs with my family are of being allowed to drink some cider with my meal (I have lived in the South far too long now to think of burnt sausages and chicken drumsticks as a "barbecue"). I am originally from the United Kingdom, where there is less of a taboo around giving children small amounts of alcohol, whether it is beer, cider or wine, usually diluted with a splash of water or some lemonade. This was how we learned to appreciate the flavors of the drinks and that those kinds of drinks are not reserved for adults and to be locked away in a cabinet, illicit, taboo, and therefore exciting and enticing; they were just part of life.

As a young man, moving to a major English city for college, I would have considered myself a beer drinker, but whenever summer rolled around, I hankered for pints of cider in the pubs I went to. As I was a younger man, I can't say that the ciders I was drinking were great examples of the English cider-making traditions that you find in the West Country or in the East of England. They were well-known brands; let's leave it at that.

My introduction, though, to cider in Virginia—when I still had to remember to add the epithetical adjective *hard* to a drink that I didn't know could be nonalcoholic—came on the very day my wife and I drove from her parents' place in South Carolina to our new home in Charlottesville, Virginia, in July 2009.

Driving up Route 29, we had just crossed the county line from Nelson County to Albemarle County when I spotted a sign for Albemarle CiderWorks. Instinctively, I knew that we would be visiting as soon as possible. A week or two later, we took the drive down to North Garden in order to investigate the first cidery to open in Central Virginia in many a long year; its official opening had taken place literally a few weeks before we moved to the area. My first experience of Virginia cider in general and Albemarle CiderWorks in particular was in their original tasting room, long before they built the delightfully light-filled extension and patio area that make any trip to North Garden even more pleasant, especially when the heat of summer has finally died off and the trees are laden with fruit waiting to become next year's vintage.

Our tasting was presided over by Charlotte Shelton, and as she walked us through the ciders they had available—Jupiter's Legacy and Royal Pippin were definitely featured—I took a mental note of the fact that she never once used the term *hard cider*. We also had a discussion about the glories of the Bramley's Seedling, an apple I maintain to this day is the finest cooking apple in human history. Having bought several bottles to take home for the fridge, I turned to Charlotte and said, "Thank you for only using the term *cider* during our tasting," to which she responded, "What else would I call it?" I knew then that Albemarle CiderWorks would become a fixture in my wife's and my world, a place we'd visit often and bring guests to as well.

It has been a pleasure, then, to see the cider world in Virginia grow in the years we have lived and set down our own roots here. A couple of years later, Potter's Craft Cider started popping up on draught in the pubs I frequented, and in their Farmhouse Dry, I found another cider to love. What had been a rarity when we arrived in 2009 was starting to gain momentum as more people passionate about apples and the ciders you can make with them started opening their own operations.

Spring forward a few more years, and we found ourselves way up in the mountains of Highland County, in Monterey, for the annual traditional music camp that my wife attends and I tag along for. It was here we discovered Big Fish Cider and fell in love with Highland Scrumpy in particular. Now, going to Big Fish is an essential part of "fiddle camp" for me, to enjoy their quite frankly superb ciders and recover from the switchbacks on Route 250, as well as take the opportunity to restock the fridge.

When, inevitably, my wife and I decided it was time to buy a house with a decent plot of land, I knew that I wanted to grow apple trees in our backyard.

I still struggle to refer to it as an orchard, though as my thirteen trees are considerably more than the bare minimum of five, I guess it is. Each of my trees has come from Vintage Virginia Apples, and most are cider varieties; of course, I have a Virginia Hewes Crab, a Harrison, a Parmar and, yes, a Bramley's Seedling.

In researching this book and visiting the cideries I profile here, I have made discoveries about cider makers doing amazing things with the humble apple, creating ciders that have literally been revelations, inspiring me to add yet another tree to my backyard grove. In this book, I also offer a list of ciders that I have either discovered or, in several instances, rediscovered as a result of spending weekends driving around the state, from the far southwest to Alexandria, from Richmond back to the rolling hills of the Piedmont. Virginia is a state with a wealth of great ciders that deserve to be appreciated among the cognoscenti of craft cider.

The history of Virginian cider might seem somewhat distant to us now, especially when we consider that apple trees and seeds arrived with the colonists in 1607 and have been used for making cider since at least the 1610s, but as I drive around the state, I am amazed at how that history surrounds us constantly. There are innumerable streets in Virginia with names like Orchard Lane—or the very specific Apple Orchard Lane in Troutville—and there are several Pippin Streets across the state, as well as a Cider House Road, likely because of what used to be there: reminders (albeit subtle) that the apple and cider making are essential to Virginian history.

Chapter 1

THE PAST

COLONIAL ERA AND EARLY UNITED STATES, 1607–1826

Aboard those three ships that sailed into the Chesapeake, and subsequent resupply missions, came apple seeds, as well as seedling trees, often planted in wooden barrels, ready to be planted out on arrival in Virginia. While it is true that there were some crab apples already native to Virginia, the English colonists brought with them the varieties they knew and trusted. It seems, though, that those European cultivars did not readily adapt to the soils and conditions of the New World—other than Ashmead's Kernel, that is, the only apple variety traceable to prerevolutionary America that is known to have come from England originally.

Yet it is also true that within twenty-five years of its establishment, Jamestown had thriving apple orchards that were able to provide the apples needed for making cider. As mentioned earlier, an apple seed will not grow a tree that produces fruit with the exact characteristics of the apple from which it came—or, to use the proper term, true to type. It was this fact that led to the birth of many of the American cider varieties we know today, especially those with recorded history in the colonial era.

That's not to say that these early English colonists relied on chance seedlings. It is recorded, for example, that in 1621, the ship *Supply* sailed for the Berkeley Hundred, a plantation of some eight thousand acres on the northern bank of the James River. Aboard the *Supply*, one John Smyth sent to the plantation "a great number of the young stocks and of apple trees grafted with pippens, pearmaynes and the other best apples."[1]

In 1644, then royal governor Sir William Berkeley, as part of his efforts to diversify the Virginian economy away from an overdependence on tobacco, decreed that for each five hundred acres granted to a planter, he must "enclose and fence a quarter-acre of ground near his dwelling house for orchards and gardens."

The apple and cider, by virtue of the love of a drink that was common to all Englishmen, whether gentleman adventurer, tradesman or lowly servant, were firmly at the heart of colonial Virginia within a few decades of those Englishmen first setting foot in their New World.

Once orchards were established and cider production began in earnest, we find Virginia cider becoming a small-time export commodity. While it was not a common feature of the trade between the colony of Virginia and the English motherland, there are records of larger-scale planters exporting Virginia cider back to England, including William Fitzhugh. When Fitzhugh exported some of his cider to England, he declared that the cider produced from his orchard of 2,500 trees was equivalent in value to 15,000 pounds of tobacco. The price per pound of tobacco in the 1670s hovered around one and a half pence, which would make the value of his cider 22,500 pennies, or £93 and 8 shillings in pounds sterling at the time, roughly the equivalent of $22,000 in 2024 dollars.[2]

It is clear, therefore, that in the nascent economy of early colonial Virginia, cider played a far more important role than just something to slake one's thirst. Cider provided hydration in the absence of easily available drinking water and nutrition in the form of readily available vitamins. Like many alcoholic drinks developed by various cultures, regardless of place and time, cider was a way of preserving a crop and having something valuable at hand with which to trade. The colonial economy at the time was not a simple cash economy but rather one where bartering was part and parcel of daily life.

In surviving letters from the early eighteenth century, we find requests for sizable amounts of cider from members of the planter class, such as Arthur Allen, who at one time owned more than ten thousand acres in Surry County, on the south side of the River James. In July 1704, Allen sent a letter to a John Owen reminding him of a transaction in which Allen had agreed to "have twenty hhds [hogsheads, barrels with a volume of about fifty-eight gallons] filled with very good Cyder for you by the last of ye next month."

Clearly, though, as Allen goes on to mention, the previous year's arrangement had not been to his satisfaction. He continues:

> *I thought fitt to give you this early notice yt* [that] *you mought make provision to fetch it at ye very time, but do assure you if after I have done my part you fail to doe yours & the Cyder receives any injury you must not expect me to bear any part of the loss having been too much prejudiced on that acct last year.*[3]

Obviously, a slightly strained relationship between supplier and distributor is nothing new. The wealthy planter class regularly supplied tavernkeepers with cider, as well as other surplus from their plantations. William Byrd II (1674–1744), who had the mansion at Westover Plantation built in the 1740s, is known to have supplied cider to Susannah Allen for her Williamsburg tavern, while her fellow Williamsburg tavern owner Anne Pattison sourced her cider from the Carter's Grove plantation, seat of the Burwell family. In the taverns of Virginia, though, not only would cider be served straight, but it also formed the basis of other drinks, sometimes being spiked with hard liquor to give the cider a little extra oomph.

The connection between drunkenness, cider and rebellion was made by Nicholas Spencer after Bacon's Rebellion in 1676, which he claimed was caused by "all plantations flowing with sydcr, soc unripe drank by our licentious inhabitants, that they allow no tyme for its fermentation but in their braines."[4]

Even so, cider was part and parcel of everyday life for the colonists of Virginia, and the first cookbook to be published in colonial America contains directions to make cider. Eliza Smith's *The Compleat Housewife* was originally published in London in 1727; the American version was published in Williamsburg in 1742 and gives us insight into how cider, spelled "cyder," would have been made. To begin with, Smith writes, "pull your fruit before it is too ripe, and let it lie but one or two days.…Your apples must be pippins, pearmains, or harveys."[5]

Smith also recommends not mixing early ripening apples with late season fruit. Having chopped and pressed the apples, the juice is to be put into a hogshead, with "three or four pound of raisins…and two pound of sugar."[6]

The addition of sugar to the cider would have increased the alcohol content, a fact that we are very aware of today, but in the early eighteenth century, there was very little understanding of the workings of yeast, hence Smith's comment that the sugar "will make it work better." Raisins were added to the cask to help the fermentation, though it is unlikely that cider makers of the day understand that raisins contain essential nutrients for yeast and also add some additional tannins to the cider in order to improve the body and mouthfeel.

Finally, Smith explains the process of racking, or moving the cider off the lees into smaller vessels in order to fine the cider and make it clear, the last step being to "bottle it in *March*."[7]

As we come closer to the decades leading up to the American Revolution, we see that cider is deeply entrenched in Virginian society, including being offered as remuneration for plantation overseers; for instance, when Edward Mundford employed Turner Jackson in 1760, their agreement included "one full share of the crop, cider, and every tenth hog."[8]

Cider was of such value that it even turns up in notices of sale of the property of the deceased, such as when one Richmond Terrell died in 1771. In publicizing the sale of his estate, the executors of the will announced in the *Virginia Gazette* that the property included "some brandy and cider."[9]

In the orchards of Virginia, several of the apple varieties used in the modern cider industry were already developing their reputations as cider apples during this period. Cider was also being used as a tool for political persuasion. When George Washington ran for office in the colonial House of Burgesses in 1758, he paid for more than 140 gallons of cider and beer to be provided to the electorate of Frederick County in the hope that such generosity would convince them to send him to Williamsburg, then capital of Virginia. It must have worked: Washington would represent Frederick County in the House of Burgesses until 1765, when he was elected to represent Fairfax County, a seat that he would retain until the outbreak of the Revolutionary War in 1775.

As a member of the planter class, Washington was an avid gardener, growing apples in the gardens at Mount Vernon as well as at his outlying farms. In 1763, he recorded grafting forty-three "Maryland Red Strick," the scion wood coming from one William Digges. That same year, he grafted ten "New Town Pippin," which he had received from then acting governor of Virginia John Blair.[10] As well as growing apple trees with which to produce his own cider, Washington is recorded buying it in several times, one such occasion being in October 1768, when he ordered two barrels of "crab-apple cider" from a distant cousin, John Washington.[11]

It is also clear from Washington's own diary entries that he practiced an ancient form of apple cultivation, using apple pomace as a mulch along fence lines. In an entry from October 1768, Washington notes that on that day they had "Sowed Apple Pummice in the New Garden—from Crab Apples."[12] The seeds in the pomace would sprout, and the resulting trees could either be used as a source of rootstock to graft known varieties onto or, if providence shined upon them, become a new seedling tree with apples that had the right balance of sugar, acid and tannin to make more cider.

We also know that Washington traded cider with fellow planters in the northern reaches of Virginia, such as George Mason of Gunston Hall, who in late 1785 "broach'd four or five hogsheads of Cyder, & filled your Bottles with what we thought the best." At this time, Mason was using almost exclusively the Maryland Red Streak apple for his cider, and he noted in his letter to Washington:

> *As the Cyder in the Bottles will not ripen, fit for use, 'til late in May, I have also filled a Barrel, out of the same Hhd. which I beg your acceptance of. If you use it out of the barrel, you will find it (as all sweet Cyder is) much more grateful to the Stomack, by having a little Ginger grated upon it.*[13]

In central Virginia, it is known that Thomas Jefferson was growing Virginia Hewes Crab, Roxbury Russet and Albemarle Pippin in the orchards at Monticello in the years leading up to the Revolution. Jefferson's friend and advisor Dr. Thomas Walker of the Castle Hill plantation is said to have become a fan of the Newtown Pippin while serving with George Washington in the Continental army. On his return from the Battle of Brandywine in 1777, Walker brought with him scions of Newtown Pippin, which would become so popular in Albemarle County that it eventually became synonymous with the county as the Albemarle Pippin, though that name would not be recorded in nursery stock lists until the middle of the nineteenth century.

Although cider was produced in prodigious amounts throughout colonial Virginia and was a cause of consternation to the political classes at times, as we have seen, cider was also imported from Great Britain. This fact, though, meant that cider was caught up in the growing tensions between the colonies and the mother country, with the House of Burgesses resolving to no longer "directly or indirectly, import, or cause to be imported" a considerable list of commodities, including cider.[14]

During the ensuing eight years of the Revolutionary War, cider was considered part of the soldier's ration in the Continental army: each soldier was entitled to a quart of either cider or spruce beer, depending on what was available to the commissariat. Once the war came to its end and the now United States of America set about building the new nation that had been won, cider in Virginia picked up where it had left off, as the everyman's drink.

It was in this postrevolutionary world that the likes of Thomas Jefferson would conduct the business of cider making with all their penchant for recordkeeping and information sharing. Recalling his life to Dr. Vine Utley, Jefferson noted that "malt liquors and cider are my table drinks," pointing to the prominent role that cider played in daily life at Monticello.

When it came to cider making, though, Jefferson particularly enjoyed the Virginia Hewes Crab, which he described as a "common apple on the James River" in a letter to James Mease of the Philadelphia Society for Promoting Agriculture, and a lost variety of apple called Taliaferro (pronounced "tol-iver").[15] In describing the cider produced from the Taliaferro, Jefferson extolled its virtues in a letter to his granddaughter, Ellen Wayles Randolph Coolidge:

> They are called the Taliaferro apple, being from a seedling tree, discovered by a gentleman of that name near Williamsburg, and yield unquestionably the finest cyder we have ever known, and more like wine than any liquor I have ever tasted which was not wine.[16]

It is through Jefferson's writings that we get a glimpse of one of the key aspects of plantation life that is often overlooked in popular histories: the

An ancient style of agricultural fork, formed by forcing a tree to grow in such a way as to have three distinct tines.

centrality of the enslaved community of Virginia to the production of the cider. As was true of any agricultural labor in this period, the overwhelming majority of people in the orchards, crushing the apples, pressing the juice and eventually bottling the end product, cider, were of African descent. This was particularly true on the large estates of the planter class.

Central to the cider-making concern at Monticello was an enslaved man by the name of Jupiter Evans. Jupiter's life was intimately intertwined with that of Jefferson. Jupiter was born in the same year as Jefferson on the Shadwell property of Jefferson's father, Peter, and when Jupiter reached the age of twenty-one, Peter Jefferson transferred ownership of Jupiter to his son Thomas. The younger Jefferson made Jupiter his personal valet, as well as having him work as a stonecutter and look after his horses and coaches. It would also seem that Jupiter was central to Monticello's cider-making activities, as were George Granger and his wife, Ursula.

The Grangers were purchased by Jefferson in the years leading up to the Revolutionary War, and at least by 1787, George was in charge of Jefferson's orchards, meaning that he was integral to making the cider as well. In his Farm Book, Jefferson noted that in November 1799, his orchards had produced

> *70. bushels of the Robinson & red Hughes (about half of each)* [that] *have made 120. gallons of cyder. George says that when in a proper state (there was much rot among these) they ought to make 3. galls. to the bushel, as he knows from having often measured both.*[17]

The "Robinson" apple mentioned here is an alternative name for the Taliaferro apple that Jefferson believed made the finest cider he had ever tasted. It would appear that Ursula had also long been involved in the annual bottling of the cider, which took place in March each year once the apple harvest had fermented. Within a few months of each other, Jupiter Evans and George Granger died, victims of a sickness that swept through Monticello in the winter of 1799–1800, and Jefferson sent instructions to his son-in-law, Thomas Mann Randolph: "I must get Martha or yourself to give orders for bottling the cyder in the proper season in March. There is nobody there but Ursula who unites trust & skill to do it. She may take any body she pleases to aid her."[18]

Subsequently, Jefferson rarely mentions cider in his writings, other than an 1817 imprecation to his then overseer Edmund Bacon to have cider made with the Hewes Crab from the North Orchard:

We have saved red Hughes enough from the North orchard to make a smart cask of cyder. They are now mellow & beginning to rot. I will pray you therefore to have them made into cyder immediately. Let them be made clean one by one, and all the rotten ones thrown away or the rot cut out. Nothing else can ensure fine cyder.[19]

George Washington also relied on the labor of the enslaved in tending his orchards along the Potomac, as well as pressing the harvest for cider. The Mount Vernon plantation, some eight thousand acres, consisted of five distinct farms, Dogue Run, Mansion House, Muddy Hole, River Farm and Union Farm, each with its overseer reporting up to an overall plantation manager. The overseer of each farm was tasked with bringing in the cider, and on several occasions, that overseer was part of the enslaved community, including Israel Morris at Dogue Run from 1766 to 1794. Davy Gray was the overseer at Muddy Hole from 1770 until Washington's death in 1799, other than when he was the overseer at River Farm from 1785 to 1792.

It is also well known that many enslaved people practiced sidelines in growing fruit and making alcoholic beverages to sell to non-enslaved Virginians, potentially including free people of color, at least one of whom, Petersburg barber and entrepreneur William Colson, was shipping cider from Virginia to Liberia in Africa in the early nineteenth century.[20] We can also find evidence of enslaved and free people of color growing apples, presumably for making cider, in the use of the word "Aunt" in the name of a given variety. Examples of this are the Aunt Cora's Field Apple and the Aunt Cora's Yard Apple, which Cora's father grew from seed while he was enslaved in Bath County to a master noted for his cruelty.

As well as being intimately involved in every step of the cider-making process, from tending to the orchards to pressing the fruit, placing the must into barrels and eventually bottling the end product, enslaved people also enjoyed drinking cider, as well as other alcoholic beverages. It is true that drinks in general are rarely mentioned in accounts of rations provided to enslaved communities, but given that cider was essentially a commodity during this period, it is highly likely that the enslaved commonly drank cider, especially at celebrations such as Christmas, which, according to a popular rhyme,

comes but once a year;
Every man must have his sheer
Of apple cider'n 'simmon beer.[21]

The Past

INDUSTRIALIZATION AND PROHIBITION, 1825–1945

As the Founding Fathers started to pass away, Virginia's love of cider remained strong, though it would not be long before the headwinds of change began to buffet the established order.

Throughout the 1830s, though, Virginians clearly cared enough about the quality of the cider they produced for several newspapers in the commonwealth to publish treatises from other newspapers about how to make the best possible cider. In syndicating an article from the *Northern Star*, a newspaper in Rhode Island, the August 30, 1830 edition of the *Lynchburg Virginian* encouraged cider makers that

> *it is requisite that the apples should be perfectly sound, but mellow: that great care should be taken in having every thing belonging to the cider mill clean with a cleanly disposition in those about it, and lastly, the cider, well strained, should be put into clean casks and conveyed to the cellar.*[22]

The article continues to remind the cider maker that it is important to seal the casks before fermentation has finished, referred to as "nicking," sealing in the remaining carbon dioxide created through the action of the yeast; at the time, this was referred to as "fixed air." It was clearly understood that sealing in the "fixed air" before fermentation was fully complete would also add sparkle to the cider: "The object of nicking is to prevent escape of the fixed air, which gives the sparkling appearance & lively taste that always belong to good cider."[23]

It is also evident that during this period, Virginians understood cider to be more akin to wine than any other alcoholic beverage:

> *This is a point that deserves great attention. Cider, when properly managed is in the condition of wine—in fact, it is a sort of moderate wine—and the object is to prevent it becoming vinegar. Too great care therefore, cannot be taken to keep the fixed air in, and the atmospheric air out.*[24]

It was common throughout the 1830s and 1840s to see cider offered for sale through the newspapers, including specifically Virginia cider.[25]

Perhaps the height of cider in the popular consciousness would arrive with the 1840 presidential election, when a glib comment by a Democratic newspaper claimed that Whig candidate William Henry Harrison would sit "by the side of a 'sea-coal' fire, and study moral philosophy" if given a "barrel of hard cider." Harrison seized on this to present a rootsy image, which led to the 1840 election being known as the "Log Cabin and Hard Cider" election.

Virginians in the traditional cider-producing regions along the Blue Ridge Mountains and in northern Virginia clearly found the image of Harrison as a cider-drinking frontiersman appealing, as they voted decisively for him, though overall he would lose the popular vote in Virginia by a little less than 1.5 percent. This was likely cider's apogee in the public mind, as lurking in the changes society was experiencing was the downfall of hard cider as the drink of choice among Virginians.

As early as 1800, movements committed to temperance, the belief that alcohol is bad for society, were established in Virginia. Initially their targets were the strong liquors, such as corn whiskey and apple brandy; indeed, drinks like cider and beer were presented as the temperance alternative to such deleterious spirits. As time wore on, though, the temperance movement morphed into campaigns for outright prohibition, and so cider became a target of organizations such as the Woman's Christian Temperance Union, which founded a chapter in Virginia in 1883, and the Anti-Saloon League, which started in 1901.

Around this same period, accelerated by Reconstruction as a result of the end of the Civil War in 1865, more and more people were moving from rural Virginia into growing urban areas such as Richmond, Alexandria, Petersburg and Norfolk. With a population of recently freed people of color also migrating from rural Virginia in search of work and opportunity, it seemed that cider's days as Virginia's common drink were numbered. As was common in many countries during the Industrial Revolution, once people lost the connection to the land, agrarian—and seasonal—products like cider lost popularity, supplareplacements that could be produced year-round.

While it is true that urbanization in Virginia was slower than in the rest of the United States, the process was well underway, and the newly urbanized working classes turned to a new drink to slake their thirst: lager beer.

While beer had been very much part of Virginia's drinking culture and rivaled cider as the drink of choice, it was most often made at home. It was only in the decades following a wave of German immigration into urban centers like Richmond and Alexandria that industrial-scale beer brewing came to Virginia. Writing about Richmond in 1860, Samuel P. Day commented that "a large proportion of the inhabitants are Germans, who either keep lager-beer saloons, or clothing stores."[26]

With such a large German population, importing German-style lager beer was big business, with adverts in German-language newspapers such as *Richmonder Anzeiger* touting arrivals of lager from the homeland or more established German centers in the North. In the aftermath of the Civil War, David G. Yeungling Jr. of the Pennsylvania brewing dynasty opened the largest brewery in Richmond at the time, the James River Steam Brewery.

The James River Steam Brewery brewed ale and porter as well as lager beer, in an effort to appeal to as broad an audience as possible. With the financial woes of the 1870s, Yuengling admitted defeat and closed his brewery, but the demand for beer among the urban working classes remained and would eventually be met by large national brewing companies establishing a foothold in Richmond. By the turn of the twentieth century, Richmond was home to branches of such established lager breweries as Anheuser-Busch, Schlitz and Pabst, as well as a clutch of locally owned breweries, including Peter Strumpf's Home Brewing Company.[27]

The 1870s saw a major technological advance that gave industrial-scale lager production in the United States a major advantage over the more agrarian cider world: the invention and use of refrigeration, in particular refrigerated rail cars. Artificial refrigeration had existed since William Cullen built the first refrigerating machine in 1755, but it hadn't yet found any commercial purpose. It was the Frenchman Ferdinand Carré who created the first commercially viable ice-making machine.[28]

The boom in lager brewing across the United States, as well as Virginia, made the new lager brewers early and enthusiastic adopters of the new technologies in refrigeration, as it lessened their dependance on ice from the northern states and the need for extensive underground tunnels in which to lager their beer. These early adopters of refrigeration in the brewing industry further cemented their growing dominance in the alcoholic drinks market by making use of the refrigerated rail cars invented by Detroit's William David, meaning their products could reach a far broader market while remaining fresh.[29] Where the railways went, lager beer was quick to follow.

At the same time as industrial-scale brewing was becoming prevalent throughout Virginia, the cause of cider was not helped by an impetus among agricultural thought leaders at the time advocating for the improving of farming methods and output. The influential agricultural journal the *Southern Planter* claimed in 1857 that "the farmers of Virginia, in general, have cultivated the apple only for making cider, vinegar, and brandy, and as a consequence, there are but few orchards of good apples in the State, and those planted at a comparatively recent period."[30]

While the *Planter*'s editors went on to claim that they had no wish to devalue growing apples for cider, they concluded, "We shall take occasion at another time to prove that it will pay better to raise finer apples, such as can be packed in barrels and sold in the markets.…We are extremely anxious to promote the cultivation of the better varieties in Virginia."

With even the worthies of agriculture seemingly setting face against cider, centuries of tradition were threatened by the many strands of "modernity" that were weaving together to create much of the Virginia we know today.

In the nineteenth century, while cider was essentially a commodity, it was also heavily seasonally dependent, as it is today. Apple picking and cider pressing are autumnal activities, and in the age before refrigeration and storage, the entire crop would have to be processed before the apples rotted away. Malted barley, on the other hand, can be stored at ambient temperatures for extended periods of time, and with the rise in German-speaking immigrants in the 1860s and '70s, Virginia's urban workers found in lager beer a regular supply of drink year-round. In the event that a cider maker sells all their product before the next harvest, that's it—they're done for the year, whereas breweries running low on beer can just make some more, giving them the inherent advantage of always being able to have product available.

Cider, therefore, suffered a double blow in the lead-up to Virginia's statewide prohibition, which came into effect at the stroke of midnight on October 31, 1916, three years before nationwide prohibition would be foisted on the American people. Firstly, cider makers lost drinkers to the newfangled lager beer, and then came the hammer blow of prohibition, as a result of which orchards had to turn to alternative uses for their crops to make up the shortfall in revenue. It was during prohibition that orchards increasingly grubbed up the flavorful crab apples and cider varieties that had been so celebrated in the previous three centuries.

In the interwar years, more and more of the orchards that once lined the Shenandoah Valley and mountainous regions of Virginia were abandoned for lack of a living from the land. In the 1920s and '30s, the Commonwealth of Virginia used its power of eminent domain to seize orchard land in the Blue Ridge Mountains to create the Shenandoah National Park. Remnants of these orchards remain throughout the park, in particular around the Milam Gap, Beagle Gap and Loft Mountain areas.

THE DOLDRUMS, 1945–1995

Despite nationwide prohibition coming to an end in 1933, there wasn't a revival in fortunes of Virginia's previously dominant cider industry. Although occurring at a slower rate than in other parts of the United States, industrialization and its attendant urbanization were unstoppable, and in 1950, more Virginians lived in the cities than in the countryside.

By this point, most of the orchards that were still in business had crossed over to growing apples for eating, packing or processing. Gone were the massed ranks of Albemarle Pippins, Winesap and Black Twig, though they hung on in smaller homestead orchards in the mountains. The commercial orchards that remained now grew popular varieties such as Golden Delicious, Granny Smith and MacIntosh, all of them lacking the proper amounts of acid and tannins needed for cider production.

While Virginia remained one of the major apple-growing regions in the country, its cider industry was no more. Much as the mythologies of old cling on in the popular imagination as fairy tales, the word *cider* became associated with freshly pressed but decidedly sweet—and unfermented—apple juice. Orchards in fall became more associated with applesauce, donuts and freshly pressed juice than the centuries of cider history that came before.

It is a motif found across the globe that as people migrate to cities in search of work and opportunities, if they don't still have a foot in the countryside, it will not take long for folk customs and wisdom to die out. Where once there were entire communities dependent on growing apples and making cider, today there are remnants of orchards left to go feral, untended and uncared for—in particular in the Shenandoah National Park, where about two thousand people were cleared from the land through the use of eminent domain to make way for the national park. Though the people were forced out of their homes, their orchards remained, and fragments of them are there to this day, especially around Milam Gap and further south at Beagle Pass.

When, in the late 1970s, the Shenandoah National Park Oral History Collection was instituted, several of the former residents of the land that formed the park were interviewed about what life had been like in the mountains. Apples and cider were a recurring theme. When interviewed for the project by Dorothy Noble Smith as part of her research for *Recollections: The People of the Blue Ridge Remember*, Homer Frazier commented, "All of us made cider." His wife, Virgie, described the cider made by her grandfather:

He made the best cider....When it just begins to get a little bit—get a few bubbles in it that's the way I like it. I don't like it real sweet, and I don't like it sour. But he'd make me wash every apple, we's helping to wash them. We'd wash every apple till it was as clean as could be, make real cider.[31]

While making cider was a feature of life for many of the people interviewed, not everyone could afford the equipment to do so; in particular, few had access to a mill and press. As such, neighbors would bring their apples to someone with a cider mill, such as the father of Cleadus Meadows: "They brought the apples and had it made....My dad would loan anything he had, I think aside from, except maybe the cider mill."[32]

Throughout the interviews, it becomes clear that by the 1930s, the transition toward understanding cider to be something more often nonalcoholic than the alcoholic drink it had been for centuries was well underway. Clearly, though, some still had the habit of letting fermentation begin, as the source of the bubbles that Virgie Frazier liked would have been the action of yeast on the sugars in the must. However, the interviews also show that there was some understanding of cider having the potential to be something else. As Zada Lam put it: "Oh, we had cider. We drank cider. Not strong cider, just sweet cider."[33]

As it had been throughout the centuries of Virginia history, cider wasn't just a drink for those of European descent: African Americans living in the mountains enjoyed cider just as much. When Noble Smith interviewed Luther and Myra Wood, they shared how cider was part and parcel of corn shucking: "It was a whole lot of boys and girls around shuckin'....Which every one got to that jug first...big jug of cider...got the first drink."[34]

Despite the continued centrality of the apple to mountain life, cider as the alcoholic beverage that was known and loved by Virginians for nearly three hundred years was, for all intents and purposes, dead—well, almost.

In the headlong rush for modernity, industrialization and urbanization, there were still people in the mountains for whom the apple was a near-mystical gift, who never forgot the names Virginia Hewes Crab, Taliaferro or Roxbury Russet. Probably the most influential of these keepers of the flame was Tom Burford.

Born in 1935 in Amherst County, Thomas Nelson Burford descended from some of the earliest settlers in Amherst and Nelson Counties, able to trace his ancestry back to the same era in Virginia as several of the apple varieties for which he would become a passionate, and forceful, advocate. Growing up on the family farm at Tobacco Row Mountain, he was surrounded by

A vintage cider press, dating from approximately the 1930s. Such presses were commonly used by people in the Blue Ridge Mountains.

apple trees from birth; he would often say that his mother went into labor with him while picking a Pennsylvania variety called Smokehouse.

With his brother, Burford ran Burford Brothers, a business comprising an orchard, tree nursery and farm as well as several other concerns, but it was his orchard and nursery that were at the heart of his life's work: to ensure that the United States in general, and Virginia in particular, didn't lose its storehouse of apple-growing treasure.

In the early 1980s, Burford worked with Peter Hatch at Monticello to re-create Jefferson's North Orchard, as Burford's own orchards contained many of the same trees that Jefferson had planted. The North Orchard was Jefferson's dedicated apple and peach orchard, very much in the style of the "farm orchard" that was a feature of many a homestead at the time. Planted mostly with Virginia Hewes Crab and Taliaferro, Jefferson's North Orchard, being in the farm orchard style, would not have been immaculately tended, unlike his South Orchard, since the primary purpose of the fruit was to be turned into cider. The collaboration of Hatch and Burford in re-creating the North Orchard would become a turning point for cider apples and, consequently, cider in Virginia.

Virginia's modern cider industry is indebted to Burford not only for restoring the Virginia Hewes Crab to Monticello but also for his discoveries of several older American cider apples that were thought lost. Notable among these is the Harrison: on rediscovering it in New Jersey, Burford allegedly had to take a seat, he was so overcome. Rediscovering Harrison was more than just an obsession for Tom Burford; it had been so for his father as well. Of the new generation of cider makers in Virginia, nearly all use the Harrison, and in Chuck Shelton of Albemarle CiderWorks the variety has a committed champion. "Harrison is the best cider apple in the world," Shelton has said. "It has more acid, more tannins, and more sugar than other varieties."[35]

Burford's work also resulted in the magisterial *Apples of North America: Exceptional Varieties for Growers, Gardeners and Cooks*, published in 2013. The book is a guide to more than 150 varieties of apple grown in the United States, many of them storied heirloom varieties that make good cider.

For many years, Tom taught the art of tree grafting, and it was this work that, perhaps more than any other, laid the roots for the revival of traditional cider that Virginia revels in today. Students of Burford's include the Sheltons, who initially established Vintage Virginia Apples, better known today as Albemarle CiderWorks, and Diane Flynt of Foggy Ridge Cider.

Rejuvenation, 1995–2023

Foggy Ridge Cider, located in Dugspur, Carroll County, in the very southwest of Virginia, was the first modern cider maker in Virginia when it opened in 1997. With a longing to leave behind the hustle and bustle of a career in banking, Diane Flynt established Foggy Ridge as an orchard focused on growing classic American cider varieties, which she and her team would then press into traditional-style ciders, where the fruit itself is central.

In 1995, Diane and her husband, Chuck, purchased the farm in Carroll County, deep in Southwest Virginia, sandwiched between North Carolina and West Virginia, where the Blue Ridge Mountains form the eastern edge of Appalachia. This part of Virginia has long been apple country, with commercial orchards still lining the mountains and valleys, many of them in the hands of families that have grown apples here for generation after generation.

Diane comments in her 2023 book *Wild, Tamed, Lost, Revived* that, in trying to decide what to do with the farm, "growing vegetables for the local farmers' market or starting a perennial nursery didn't strike a chord with me. Trees seemed more significant than decorative flowers, more enduring than vegetables. With trees I could grow something that would produce and outlive me, a fruitful legacy."[36]

At the time, Virginia's wine industry was in the early stages of development, and the commonwealth's Department of Agriculture was running several programs to support this growing industry. It was then that Diane decided she would start an orchard focused on traditional cider apples and also make cider from them; thus Foggy Ridge Cider was born.

Diane and Chuck named their orchard and cidery Foggy Ridge for the mist that, nearly every morning, rises off Rock House Creek, which runs through the farm. The mist blankets the mountains, wending its way through the orchards in which traditional cider apples grow. When Diane was in the planning stages of setting up Foggy Ridge, she naturally came into the orbit of Tom Burford, who provided invaluable advice about how to lay out her orchards and, most importantly, which varieties to grow. Unsurprisingly, perhaps, Burford recommended that Harrison be a central feature of the orchard.

When it came to producing the kind of ciders she had envisioned, Diane experienced all the trial and error that can make producing alcohol at home so frustrating. Describing those early batches of homemade cider, she notes,

"My tasting notebook was full of descriptors like 'rotten eggs,' 'burnt rubber,' 'airplane glue,' and 'Band-Aids'…not the cider I had in mind."[37]

Eventually, though, Diane got a handle on the relationships between the apples going into the press and the flavors of the juice that would eventually become cider. In the fall of 2003, Foggy Ridge did their first full-scale pressing, blending Virginia Hewes Crab, Parmar, Smith Cider, Ribston Pippin and Grimes Golden.

Now making cider that she was happy with, Diane set about perhaps the greatest challenge she'd yet faced as the first cider maker in Virginia for generations: restoring cider to its original place in the hearts and minds of drinkers. The challenge was less about getting people to try traditional cider and more about getting them to buy it regularly. From 2003 until its final vintage in 2017, Foggy Ridge set the standard of what Virginia cider could be: made exclusively with cider apples, with a deep focus on harvesting and pressing at the appropriate times to ensure the balance of sugars, acids and tannins was just right.

Around the same time as Diane was planting the orchards at Foggy Ridge, Charlotte Shelton and her brother Chuck attended apple-tasting events hosted at Monticello by Tom Burford and Peter Hatch, which resulted in the Sheltons starting to plant heirloom apple varieties at the family farm in North Garden. Among those early trees in the orchard was Virginia Hewes Crab, grafted from scion wood that came from the North Orchard at Monticello.

Initially interested in growing heirloom trees, the Sheltons needed to find something to do with their growing orchard, which had expanded to over two hundred distinct varieties. They had done some direct sales of apples, taught grafting with Tom Burford and, eventually, sold trees through their online catalog. Eventually, though, they decided to go one step further and start a cidery, which they did in 2009 when then governor of Virginia Tim Kaine officially opened Albemarle CiderWorks.

At first, Albemarle CiderWorks produced just three ciders: two blends, Jupiter's Legacy and Ragged Mountain, and a single varietal fermentation of Albemarle Pippins, Royal Pippin. Like Diane Flynt at Foggy Ridge, Albemarle CiderWorks focuses on creating traditional Virginia ciders, made mainly with historic cider apples, though they are not averse to dabbling in a little experimentation. It is difficult to overstate the influence that the Sheltons, both Charlotte and Chuck, have had on the cider industry that has blossomed across Virginia in the decade and a half since Albemarle CiderWorks opened.

For example, it was as a result of attending Chuck's cider makers' forums that Kirk Billingsley of Big Fish Cider in Highland County realized that the cider he was making was in the same vein as those for which Albemarle CiderWorks is rightly renowned. Kirk likewise planted orchards, using trees purchased from Albemarle CiderWorks, and in 2016 opened his own tasting room in Monterey, selling his mountain cider that has gone on to win awards and receive plaudits.

Albemarle CiderWorks has also received international attention and is well regarded by cider makers in Europe, none more so than perhaps the single most influential cider maker in England today, Tom Oliver, who describes it as being "the real deal, the whole package, and one of the best finds in cider I have come across."[38]

In the fifteen years since then governor, now senator Kaine opened Albemarle CiderWorks, there has been a flowering of cideries in Virginia. Where once there was a handful of pioneers growing obscure, long-forgotten trees and making ciders rooted in the Jeffersonian era, today there are more than thirty dedicated cideries in Virginia. These cideries run the gamut from traditional American cider—inspired by the traditions of England, France and Spain—to modern flavored ciders, drawing influence from the craft beer industry that likewise boomed in the 2010s.

In addition to the cider makers for whom the apple is the core of their work, cider is also being produced by several breweries and wineries throughout Virginia as they seek to add cider to their offerings.

Chapter 2

THE PRESENT

Apples in Virginia Cider

This is in no way whatsoever an exhaustive list of the apple varieties being used to make cider in Virginia today, partly because I am convinced that such a list would take a lifetime to compile. Consider, also, the fact that several cider makers in the commonwealth of Virginia use wild and feral apples to make cider, and such trees are either unknown to classification or had names that are now long forgotten, as the knowledge died out without being passed along.

This list describes the apple varieties that form the bedrock of the Virginia cider industry and are the most common that the cider lover will come across as they discover this rich world. As a caveat, while the apples themselves provide the tannins, sugars and acid that go into the cider, it is important to remember that both the skill of the cider maker and the conditions in which the tree that bore the fruit grew will impact the end product. A cider made with Virginia Hewes Crab grown in the Piedmont region will taste distinctly different from one using apples that grew at higher elevations or even those that grow in the warmer reaches of Southwest Virginia, where spring comes earlier.

Albemarle Pippin

Also known as the Newtown Pippin and first recorded in the early years of the eighteenth century in New York, the Newtown Pippin, according to legend and tradition, made its way to central Virginia by way of Dr. Thomas Walker, who owned the Castle Hill plantation in Albemarle County. He planted several Newtown Pippins in his orchard, and in time, the variety became synonymous with Albemarle County, being a favorite of Thomas Jefferson as well. Newtown Pippins also found their way into the orchards of George Washington in the 1760s at the latest, though it was Pippins from the Enniscorthy plantation near Scottsville that were to bring the variety to a wider, aristocratic audience. In 1838, Andrew Stevenson, then ambassador to the United Kingdom, presented Queen Victoria with a basket of Albemarle Pippins. So taken with the apples was Victoria that she saw to it that import levies on Albemarle Pippins were waived, and the apple enjoyed great popularity in the United Kingdom as a result.

Arkansas Black

There are few apples as striking as the Arkansas Black, with its deep purple skin that has more in common with black cherries than most people's perception of an apple. Thought to be a seedling from a Winesap tree, given its similarities to that family of apple, Arkansas Black is notably aromatic and produces cider with subtle tannins and usually a fine crisp finish. Albemarle CiderWorks and Blue Bee Cider both make single varietal ciders with this apple variety.

Ashmead's Kernel

The variety is unique in being popular, and productive, on both sides of the Atlantic. Ashmead's Kernel was one of the few cultivars that early colonists brought with them from England and that thrived in the soils of America; the vast majority of early American apple varieties were chance seedlings. Ashmead's Kernel is one of the most intriguingly flavored apples, with hints of pear drops, gooseberries, melon and freshly mown hay meadows. While the apple itself will certainly not win any beauty pageants—hence you will never find it in the supermarket—its flavor and balance of sugar to acid mean it is a delightful apple for making cider, as the likes of Big Fish Cider, Courthouse Creek Cidery and Ciders from Mars have done.

Dabinett

A classic English cider apple, particularly associated with Somerset in the West Country, Dabinett is classified as a bittersweet, meaning it has more tannin than acid and thus brings additional body to ciders in which it is used. It is rarely used as a single varietal but makes a telling contribution in blends. Albemarle CiderWorks uses it in conjunction with Harrison to make a magnificent cider that brings together the best of the American and the English West Country traditions.

Dolgo Crab

The Dolgo Crabapple originated in Russia; *dolgo* means "long" in Russian and describes perfectly the elongated, bright red fruit that the tree bears. When it was first released for sale, the tree was mainly used as a source for rootstocks or as a natural windbreak. Given the extremely high levels of pectin in the fruit, it has long been used for crab apple jellies. In recent years, though, cider has begun to be made with the Dolgo Crabapple, often in blends—though in the case of Troddenvale Cider, also as a magnificent single varietal that gives full rein to the cranberry and strawberry aromas, followed by a mouth-puckeringly dry yet floral and immensely tasty cider.

GoldRush

A product of the famed Purdue University apple-breeding program, GoldRush was bred in the 1970s from a combination of Golden Delicious, Winesap, Melrose and Japanese Crab. The result was an apple that has all the characteristics of Golden Delicious but a higher acid content, making it better suited to cider production than its supermarket shelf parent. While undeniably an excellent eating apple—indeed, it is one of my own favorites—GoldRush has found a devoted following among Virginia cider makers, several of whom produce single varietal ciders with it, including Albemarle CiderWorks, Buskey Cider and Sly Clyde.

Granny Smith

This ubiquitous green apple was first discovered as a chance seedling in New South Wales, Australia, and is possibly the world's most famous apple cultivar. The characteristic tartness of the Granny Smith makes it a refreshing and clean addition to a cider blend, though there are several cideries in Virginia making single varietal ciders with it, such as Bold Rock and Blue Toad. The apple itself gives the cider a very distinct green apple flavor and aroma, as well as floral notes, such as honeysuckle and alpine meadows, as well as a slightly sharp citrus note in the finish, reminiscent of lemongrass.

Grimes Golden

When Thomas Grimes gave his name to the eponymous apple in 1804, Brooke County, in modern-day West Virginia, was still part of Virginia. Just up the road from Grimes's hometown of Fowlersville was Wellsburg, where John Chapman, better known as Johnny Appleseed, and his brother set up an apple nursery, and there is some tradition that the original seedling was from that nursery. The Grimes Golden apple was for many years the favorite among the cider makers of the Blue Ridge Mountains, as it is relatively high in sugar and packs a spicy (think coriander), lightly honeyed flavor punch. Of the ciders made using Grimes Golden today, keep a particular eye out for those from Big Fish Cider, Troddenvale Cider and Castle Hill Cider.

Harrison

Harrison is originally from New Jersey, and at one time in the early nineteenth century, single varietal cider made from Harrison was so highly prized as to cost $10 a barrel, the equivalent of $250 today. Despite its fame—and profit margins—Harrison faded into obscurity until it was rediscovered in 1976. According to Chuck Shelton at Albemarle CiderWorks, Harrison is "the best cider apple in the world. It has more tannins, more acid, and more sugar than other varieties." Ciders made with Harrison tend to display floral notes similar to citrus blossom, as well as notes of melon and a gingery spiciness. Harrison ciders also tend toward being full-bodied, with some tannins remaining in the aftertaste. Albemarle CiderWorks, Ciders from Mars and Big Fish Cider all produce excellent single varietals with the Harrison apple.

Northern Spy

Another tree that originated in New England before finding its way south to Virginia, Northern Spy is derived from a seedling in Connecticut that was brought to New York in the early nineteenth century and thence to Virginia. Northern Spy is a great all-around apple, in that you will find it used in pies and applesauce and eaten out of the hand, as well as for making fantastic ciders, which will tend to have a bright mineral character and flavors of tropical fruits and peaches, with a noticeable pepperiness in the background. Kirk at Big Fish Cider is a big fan of the Northern Spy apple and produces a single varietal to showcase its punchy flavors.

Roxbury Russet

Roxbury Russet is believed to be the oldest named apple variety in North America, originating in Roxbury, Massachusetts, in the 1640s and soon after that being propagated from scion wood in Connecticut. The Roxbury Russet is another tree that Jefferson planted at Monticello: in the South Orchard, in 1778. Generally regarded as an all-around apple, the Roxbury Russet has good sugar levels and moderate acid but a lower level of tannins, making it more suitable for cider blends than for single varietals. In terms of flavor, you can expect plenty of spiciness in a Roxbury Russet cider. The Patois Cider team are particular fans of the Roxbury Russet, using it in many of their blends, as does Sage Bird Ciderworks.

Ruby Red Crab

This is a relative newcomer to the world of Virginia cider making, but it is already making waves and becoming the star of several award-winning ciders. Many orchards use crab apple trees as a reliable source of pollination; so it is with Silver Creek Orchards, and the seedling that became Ruby Red was one such tree, tucked behind a shed. The owner of Silver Creek noticed that the seedling tree bore fruit every year, even though the apples were quite small, and that the tree had never been sprayed, so he wondered: With traditional ciders making a comeback in Virginia, would there be a market for the fruit? It turned out that Ruby Red did indeed have a good balance of acid, tannins and sugar and that the zesty grapefruit flavors that are characteristic of the apple worked well in cider. Today, Silver Creek has cultivated about three acres of Ruby Red, and cider makers such as Daring Wine and Cider Co. and Buskey Cider are using it in their ciders, with Buskey Cider's 100 percent Ruby Red cider winning the 2024 Virginia Governor's Cup Best in Show for cider.

Virginia Hewes Crab

There is perhaps no other apple variety more synonymous with cider in Virginia. With a documented history going back beyond the American Revolution, Hewes Crab has been a stalwart for more than three hundred years. Thomas Jefferson is known to have used Virginia Hewes Crab as one of his major sources of juice for cider at Monticello. In terms of flavors you can expect from a cider made with this apple, look for a bright apple note and banana and butterscotch characteristics, as well as a spiciness likened to cinnamon. Many cider makers produce single varietals, including Blue Bee Cider, Buskey and Halcyon Days.

Wickson Crab

Originating in California, this modern crab apple is either a cross of the venerable Albemarle Pippin with Esopus Spitzenberg varieties or possibly a cross of the offspring of those varieties. What is undeniable, however, is that Wickson contains a very high sugar level, up to 25 percent, which makes it an excellent source of juice for cider making, especially when taking into account the fact that it also has plenty of acid. Wickson gives flavors of lemongrass, stone fruit and pineapple to a cider, and several cider makers produce a single varietal, including Potters Craft Cider and Sage Bird Ciderworks.

Winesap

Although the Winesap was first mentioned as being suitable for cider early in the nineteenth century, its origins are lost to history. It is known that the apple was being grown and used for cider in Virginia during the colonial era; beyond that, we know very little of its background. This apple is complex, with hints of strawberry, apple blossom and even some cedarwood. With the Winesap's great combination of tannins and acid, ciders made with it are often delicately balanced. Both Potter's Craft Cider and Albemarle CiderWorks have single varietal ciders using Winesap.

Yarlington Mill

According to legend, Yarlington Mill—another classic cider apple from the English West Country—was discovered as a seedling in the late nineteenth century by a Mr. Bartlett, sprouting from a wall next to a millrace in the village of Yarlington, hence the name. It soon became a common cider apple throughout Somerset and Devon, as well as other cider-producing areas in the West of England. It is classed as a bittersweet, meaning it has more tannins than acid and thus contributes a greater amount of body and mouthfeel to the resulting cider. Ciders made with Yarlington Mill tend to showcase its deeply earthy characteristics, including tobacco, leather and spicy flavors. Of the cider makers in Virginia using Yarlington Mill, Blue Bee Cider from Richmond is probably its main advocate.

Cider Styles in Virginia

While this is a book specifically about Virginia cider, it is important to understand that each of the cider makers profiled in this section has their own inspiration for the ciders they have chosen to make. The primary inspirations for Virginia's current set of cider makers are the English and preindustrial Virginian traditions, but not exclusively. Some have drawn on French and Spanish cider culture for their inspiration, and so it serves to give a brief overview of these traditions, thus giving context for their work.

There is a clear etymological link between the English, French and Spanish words for the fermented juice of apples: *cider*, *cidre* and *sidra*, respectively.

England

While cider is made throughout the United Kingdom, when it comes to styles, there are essentially only two, both regionally specific to parts of

England, the West Country and the East of England. The main difference between the regional variations lies in the types of apples used.

West Country cider, which comes from the southwest peninsula of England, following the Severn Estuary up to the Welsh Marches, is the cider that many think of when they imagine the archetypal "English" cider. Its defining characteristic is the use of specifically cider apple varieties, most of which have high levels of tannins. West Country ciders are often very lightly carbonated, to the point of being still, and more likely to bear the name *scrumpy*, a term that generally denotes an unrefined, farmhouse-style cider, though other origins of the word have been suggested.

Cider from the East of England, an area that encompasses East Anglia and parts of the Home Counties, mainly Sussex, Kent and Essex, makes more use of dessert and culinary apples, which are not as tannic as the traditional cider varieties of the west. As a result of the relative absence of tannin in the apples, the end product is refreshingly fruit-forward, with noticeable acidity that elevates the freshness, giving the cider a lighter, more effervescent mouthfeel and a more refined character.

France

The preeminent regions for French cider making today are, as they have been for centuries, Normandy and Brittany in the northeast of France. As mentioned in the introduction, the Norman invasion of England in 1066 was deeply influential on English cider making as it brought improved apple varieties across the English Channel. Not to be forgotten, though, is the long history of cross-channel relations between Brittany and the very western tip of England—the native language of Brittany, Breton, being a very close relative of Kernow, the native, though sadly extinct, language of Cornwall.

It is difficult to really define "styles" specific to French cider since the French cider world is heavily dependent on the concept of the *pommage*, or the apple varieties that are expected in a given area's cider. Many French cider regions rely on sweet and bittersweet apples, which have comparatively low levels of acid to bring to the mix. French cider is often much lower in alcohol than other cider due to the tradition of removing yeast nutrients through the keeving process, which results in a slow fermentation, leaving residual sugar in the cider. Often, French cider is below 5 percent alcohol by volume (abv) and has a fuller mouthfeel due to the sugars left in solution; it is also invariably sparkling.

At least one Virginia cider maker found inspiration in a now extinct style of cider from Normandy that was bone-dry and created using the same methods as champagne.

Spain

The cider in Spain is pressed mainly far from the plain—in the mountainous northern regions of Asturias and the Spanish side of the Basque Country, to be precise.

Asturian cider falls into one of two camps, *sidra* or *sidra natural*. Both "styles" are required to be made with apple varieties specifically designated for cider making; therefore, it's forbidden to use eating apples. Sidra natural must be at least 5 percent abv and made without the use of carbon dioxide beyond that which is created by the fermentation itself and without any added sugar. Fermentation takes place in barrels, relying on the natural yeast present in the apples and the environment to turn the juice into cider. Sidra is similar, other than undergoing a secondary fermentation in a manner similar to champagne.

Sagardoa, to use the Basque word for cider, can only be made with one of the 115 approved apple varieties as defined by the Euskal Sagardoa, the Protected Denomination of Origin for Spanish cider in the European Union, without added sugar or extraneous carbon dioxide. Sagardoa is also required to be the product of natural fermentation, reliant on the yeast and bacterial culture of the area in which the cider is made. Basque cider is usually bottled and consumed within fifteen months of being pressed.

THE CIDER MAKERS OF VIRGINIA

The following profiles of the cider makers currently working in Virginia do not claim to constitute an exhaustive list. It is entirely possible that there are some cideries that have managed to go completely under the radar due to size or lack of an online presence.

In profiling these cider makers, I have focused, where possible, on the people behind the cider rather than reviewing the cider they make. The Virginia cider scene is an eclectic collection of individuals from diverse backgrounds, making ciders inspired by various traditions within the broader cider world: English, French, Spanish and, of course, the historic American tradition that predated industrialization and prohibition.

As I went about selecting cider makers to profile, though, I did make some decisions about which companies to include and which to leave out, the primary deciding factor being that I wanted to highlight those for whom cider is the only—or primary, by a reasonable measure—product that they produce. I am less interested in cider brands that are a simple extension of a brewery or winery, as I firmly believe that cider stands on its own two feet rather than being an add-on product as part of a larger puzzle.

It was also important to me to include those cider makers who do not have their own orchards, especially considering those in urban areas of the commonwealth. Not everyone has the capital, space or time to plant their own orchards; even a classic cider-variety apple grafted onto a dwarfing rootstock will take at least three years to bear a reliable crop. The solution to this situation is that for some cider makers, it is more expedient to lease trees from an existing orchard, to purchase apples in the varieties that they want in their cider or, in some cases, to purchase pre-pressed juice to ferment and manipulate as they see fit.

ALBEMARLE CIDERWORKS

North Garden, Albemarle County

Despite the fact that Albemarle CiderWorks opened the doors of their tasting room in July 2009, making them the oldest active cidery in Virginia, the roots of the Shelton family in the cider world run much deeper. Albemarle CiderWorks is the very definition of a family business, headed as it is by Charlotte Shelton and her younger brothers Chuck, the cider maker, and Bill, the orchardist. However, it was their parents who in 1986 purchased and set up home on the Albemarle farm, whose name, Rural Ridge Farm, is a nod to the family's ancestral pile in Hanover County, Rural Plains, also known as the Shelton House.

In the early 1990s, Charlotte started collecting heirloom apple trees, under the tutelage of family friend and legendary orchardist Tom Burford. What started out as a handful of heirloom trees soon became a few dozen and then grew to several hundred trees, lining the south-facing hillsides that lead down to Route 29. Today the orchard boasts about 250 varieties, heirloom and modern, from around the world, including English and Dutch

A glass of Albemarle CiderWorks' Royal Pippin single varietal at the tasting room in North Garden, Virginia.

varieties such as Bramley Seedling and Belle de Boskoop. The orchard was, in fact, the heart of the farm before the Sheltons decided to establish Albemarle CiderWorks in 2007 and started construction of the tasting room that would be officially opened by then governor of Virginia Tim Kaine.

Looking for something to do with their ever-growing orchard, they initially sold apples and grafted trees, but when Chuck Shelton came home to Virginia from North Carolina to become part of the family business full time, he led the charge toward fermenting freshly pressed apple juice into cider, drawing on his experience and make-do skills as a home brewer. Chuck's first ciders were pressed with a hand-cranked press and fermented in plastic buckets and carboys that any home brewer or home winemaker would instantly recognize.

Discovering a knack for making drinkable cider, Chuck set out to create ciders that lived up to his vision of "a fine quality cider," with much in common with fine wines, where the fruit itself is the star and there is no need to add flavorings or other ingredients: freshly pressed apple juice goes in, and exceptional cider comes out a few months later.[39] At the heart of many of Chuck's blends are the Harrison and Virginia Hewes Crab apples. Chuck claims that Harrison is "the best cider apple in the world," boasting more of the acid, tannins and sugars that are essential to making good cider.[40]

The majority of Albemarle CiderWorks' products are single varietal ciders, highlighting the character of particular apples such as Harrison, Virginia Hewes Crab and Royal Pippin (named for the fact that Queen Victoria so appreciated the Albemarle Pippin that she saw to it that import duties on the apple were waived). They do, however, have a selection of blends, including their flagship Jupiter's Legacy, named for the enslaved cider maker at Monticello during Thomas Jefferson's lifetime, which is made with only heirloom American cider apple varieties and varies from year to year.

Jupiter's Legacy, as well as being their flagship cider, was also one of the initial triumvirate of ciders that the Sheltons offered when they first opened the taproom in 2009, the others being Ragged Mountain and Royal Pippin. Named for the small mountain range close to Charlottesville, Ragged

Mountain is a blend dominated by Albemarle Pippin, GoldRush and Virginia Gold, though it includes several other varieties that give it a subtle sweetness, making it an exceptionally easy-to-drink cider. Royal Pippin, as mentioned previously, is a single varietal cider made with Albemarle Pippins that showcases the apple to perfection, in particular its tropical fruit notes, such as pineapple and the slight sourness of a kiwi.

Supplementing the core range of flagships and single varietals is the Cidermaker's Choice series, an ongoing selection of experimental blends and more unusual single varietal ciders, where Chuck gets to let his creativity have full rein. Whether it is a version of Pomme Mary allowed to ferment completely dry, an Anglo-American blend of Dabinett and Harrison or a medley of crab apples, each batch is a unique expression of both fruit and cider maker.

There are few more charming and delightful places to spend an afternoon drinking cider than at the Albemarle CiderWorks tasting room, set in the rolling hills of the Virginia Piedmont, whether you're having a curated tasting or drinking by the glass. The respect for the apples themselves and their expression in the cider is evident throughout, reflecting Chuck's belief that cider is a "quality product" and should be treated as such.

APOCALYPSE CIDERY AND WINERY

Forest, Bedford County

One of the youngest cideries to have opened in Virginia as part of the revival of cider in the state, Apocalypse Cidery and Winery opened its doors in the summer of 2022. Originally the cidery was located in a building that was once a home brew supply store, run by the founder of Apocalypse, Doug John.

The impetus behind moving from selling home brew supplies to making cider came largely from the fact that John's son's brewing company, Apocalypse Ale Works, was right next door. It was a common refrain among customers that their families preferred cider or wine over beer, so clearly, there was a desire for cider in the local

A pint of Legacy Hard Cider at the Apocalypse Cidery tasting room in Forest, Virginia.

community. As of 2024, Apocalypse Cidery and Winery has moved in with Apocalypse Ale Works to allow father and son to offer all their products under a single roof.

Doug's flagship cider is a blend of locally grown apples called Legacy Cider, referring to the cider traditions so common throughout central and southwest Virginia. Legacy is also used as the base cider for a range of flavored products featuring ingredients such as mango, hops and classic apple pie spices like cinnamon and clove.

APPLE ATCHA CIDER

Sperryville, Rappahannock County

Housed in the historic Estes Mill that was built next to the Thornton River in the 1830s, Apple Atcha Cider was established in the spring of 2023 by John Hallberg, who purchased the mill in 2019 with the express aim of creating a cidery—as well as a museum dedicated to the Appalachian dulcimer, a unique musical instrument that originated in Appalachia in the 1800s.

Josh worked for several breweries in Ohio and Washington, D.C., before moving to Rappahannock in the 1990s, where he started to make cider. With Virginia cider once again on the rise, it made sense for him to put his experience to good use and start a small cidery in the Blue Ridge Mountains focused on pressing heirloom apples for the kind of ciders that would have once been commonplace.

Walking into the cidery and tasting room at Apple Atcha, housed in a nineteenth-century gristmill, feels very much like stepping back in time to when stone and solid wood were the major building materials of the day. Conveniently situated just off Route 211 as it runs from Sperryville to Luray, Apple Atcha sits deep in the rural, wooded hillsides of what were once cider's heartlands.

Apple Atcha has four ciders regularly available, as well as a cyser, which is a cider with honey added prior to fermentation as a source of additional fermentable sugars. Two of the ciders are in the classic Virginian mountain vein: dry, crisp and refreshing. Coveted Pippin is made with 100 percent Albemarle Pippins, while the Farmhouse Style cider is a blend of classic American cider apples. The remaining pair of ciders have additional flavors incorporated, namely maple syrup and hops.

BACK BAY'S FARMHOUSE BREWING

Virginia Beach

Back Bay's Farmhouse Brewing is a subsidiary of Back Bay Brewing, located on the same property in Virginia Beach. Back Bay itself was established in 2018 when Charlie Burroughs and Josh Canada decided to take their ambition of running their own brewery off their list of pipe dreams discussed in a duck blind into reality. Bringing on board several other friends, they opened up in 2012, with their location being a historic farmhouse, dating to 1912, on 8.6 acres of land.

With plenty of space at hand, Back Bay's venue is very much a social hub for the broader community around this part of Virginia Beach, and as such not only cider is available but also beer, wine and, most recently, even locally roasted coffee.

Graf, a hybrid of cider and ale, at Back Bay's Farmhouse Brewing in Virginia Beach.

The ciders being produced here, however, are very much in the modern vein, with added flavors such as plum, cherry and passionfruit making appearances. They also make a cider/beer hybrid called Graf, inspired by the fictional drink in Stephen King's Dark Tower series. A.I. 1.0 Farmhouse Graf—here, the "A.I." stands for "Apple Integration"—is a fifty-fifty blend of freshly pressed apple juice and the sweet barley malt wort that is the precursor to beer, fermented together to create what's essentially an "apple ale."

BIG FISH CIDER

Monterey, Highland County

As Kirk Billingsley's a native of Highland County, in the western mountains of Virginia, his earliest memories are intimately tied up with the apple. His parents owned a small farm just outside Monterey, which included six or seven backyard apple trees. Here in the mountains, the apple tree is near ubiquitous, the landscape dotted with orchards and the occasional single tree. Some of these orchards are tended, some are wild and some are home to legendary cider apple varieties such Virginia Hewes Crab and Harrison. Many of the trees are varieties that history once knew but does no longer.

Among Kirk's father's trees were varieties like Northern Spy, Smokehouse and Grimes Golden, and each fall, his father would take the fruit to a neighboring farm to have it pressed into sweet cider. The cider was stored in a barrel on the cool side of the farmhouse. It was here that Kirk's enduring love affair with the apple, its aromas and its flavors was born. In describing his passion for the apple, Kirk comments, "I can still remember the scent hitting my nose and the flavor just exploding in my mouth. I love the taste of apples. I love the smell of the bloom."[41]

Kirk's father let him in on a little secret: the sweet cider in the barrel tasted even better after fourteen days, as by then it would have started to ferment and develop a gentle carbonation that elevated the flavors and aromas of the apples. Kirk recounts that the highlight of his day during cider season as a child was jumping off the school bus, dropping his books and running to the barrel with a glass in hand to taste the sweet nectar. After a while, Kirk's teetotal mother would insist his father dump the remains of the barrel, lest it become too alcoholic.

Eventually Kirk went away to university, and on learning that his father had not made cider ahead of a fall trip home, he purchased a couple of gallons of sweet cider. One was to be held back for the requisite fourteen days, the other to drink fresh with his father. It was an experience laced with disappointment: "It was the most tasteless, insipid stuff I'd ever had in my entire life."[42]

Thus Kirk endeavored to learn the secrets of what made the cider from the ugly apples in his father's backyard so superior in taste to the sweet cider available in the supermarket. In every spare moment, he would be found in the library, learning all he could about apple varieties and the process of making cider.

On his return to Highland County to work for a small community bank and raise his family, Kirk continued his tradition of pressing fresh cider each fall, using apples from local farms, hedgerows and the wild trees scattered through the mountains. One anniversary, Kirk's wife bought him a press, allowing him to produce more juice each fall, and his cider began to build up a devoted following, including local stores and restaurants. It was from these beginnings that Big Fish Cider would eventually come into being.

Highland County's apple crop in 1994 was remarkable, so by the time Kirk had supplied his friends and the local community with all the fresh cider they could handle, he was left with a quandary. What to do with the bushels and bushels of apples he had yet to press? Loath to let them rot, he decided to try his hand at making "hard" cider. Having become a student of pomology, he had read widely and deeply on the subject, all the while paying little heed to the sections on hard cider in his collected books. He simply wasn't interested. Still, he didn't want to waste his pile of fruit.

Come early spring in 1995, at the time of the Highland County Maple Festival, several friends were visiting when Kirk remembered that he had several gallon jugs of now fully fermented cider in his basement. Bringing up the jugs and sharing their contents with his friends, he experienced the thrill of sharing something you have made and giving yourself and your friends a bit of a buzz. Each fall thereafter, Kirk made a little hard cider.

It was about twenty years later that Kirk learned the Sheltons of Albemarle CiderWorks were hosting regular cider makers' forums. At the first such forum he attended, Kirk tried Chuck's cider and discovered that it tasted remarkably similar to his own—and so a plan was hatched to open a cidery in the western mountains of Virginia. To make this dream a reality, Kirk purchased the trees for his orchards from Vintage Virginia Apples, another business of the Sheltons'.

In 2016, Kirk and his team opened the cidery and tasting room, drawing its name from the giant neon trout that has sat atop the building they're

The iconic "big fish," a local landmark for more than fifty years, on top of the Big Fish Cider tasting room in Monterey, Highland County.

housed in since the 1960s. The "big fish" is visible from the switchbacks of US 250 as they wind their way up into Highland County.

In addition to managing two orchards, Big Fish Cider also taps into a third, laid out by the renowned Virginia pomologist Tom Burford. Situated in a region where apple trees are commonplace, Big Fish embraces the abundance of the land. Its annual release of Highland Scrumpy, initially crafted from apples donated by locals during a massive apple drive, now features select trees that consistently yield apples ideal for cider making.

For Kirk, it is the apples of his home in Highland County that have spoken to him across the years, and it is these apples whose character he seeks to highlight in his ciders. Whether it is the annual Highland Scrumpy blend, which won a Good Food Award, or one of the several varieties to have been acclaimed at GLINTCAP, the largest cider and perry (fermented pear juice) competition in the world, he is keeping alive traditional mountain hard cider and making something beautiful from fruit that the supermarkets would reject for being ugly.

BLUE BEE CIDER

Richmond

Established by Courtney Mailey as the first urban cider works in Virginia, Blue Bee Cider is named for a native Virginian pollinator, the blue orchard bee. Having worked in economic development for many years, Courtney decided that she wanted to swap the corporate grind for a bit more of an agricultural one. As such, she enrolled in Cornell's highly regarded cider school, which was followed by a year's apprenticeship with Chuck Shelton at Albemarle CiderWorks and eventually, in 2012, by the opening of Blue Bee Cider, at the time in downtown Richmond.

For a decade thereafter, Courtney and her team made classic Virginian ciders using many of the apple varieties that are synonymous with the state: Virginia Hewes Crab, Harrison and Arkansas Black. Eventually Taylor Benson became the cider maker and his partner, Mackenzie Smith, the general manager, so it was only natural that when Courtney decided the time was right to step away from Blue Bee, Taylor and Mackenzie would buy the cidery and prepare it for its next chapter, including a move from its former location in Scott's Addition to Henrico County on Bethlehem Road.

An oak barrel used for aging ciders at Blue Bee Cider's taproom in Richmond.

Both Taylor and Mackenzie joined Blue Bee in 2015 in part-time positions that gradually led to a deepening love of cider and its production, and their roles developed into senior ones within the company as a result. Having grown up in a family that was deeply into independently crafted, small-batch beverages, Taylor initially imagined that he would work in the brewing industry. However, it was a LivingSocial deal on a tour, flight and T-shirt from Blue Bee they received on moving to Richmond that gave them their first exposure to the growing world of cider.

Taylor was very eager to get a foot in the door of some kind of craft beverage company, so he sent his résumé to many of the breweries that were popping up in Richmond in the mid-2010s. Part of the interest for him—having worked in a machine shop for several years, building parts for government contracts—was that he wanted to actually see the pleasure on his customers' faces when enjoying something he had created from start to finish, rather than just sending it out the door to a nameless, faceless workshop.

Commenting on the ethos of Blue Bee Cider, Mackenzie points out that, now that she and Taylor have taken over, there is a continuation of Courtney's founding philosophy: "Blue Bee has always been small and niche, in the way that the product we make and the service we provide has always been its own thing. Because the cider is not what the general public is used to, it was important to make sure we had conversation with visitors, centering the cider."[43]

Blue Bee Cider's ultimate ethos is to appreciate the craft of cider making in and of itself and to educate both their customers and their employees about the intricacies of cider. Mackenzie notes, for example, that "all our staff, when we hire them, they've never had cider before, and when they leave, they've become cider fanatics."[44]

While Blue Bee doesn't have their own orchard, they work closely with Silver Creek Orchards in Nelson County and Glaize Apples in Winchester. However, they deliberately source only cider apple varieties from those orchards, eschewing the use of dessert or culinary apples. It is no surprise, then, that when talking about the apples he loves to work with, Taylor comments: "Being in Virginia, I do have to acknowledge Hewes Crab—it is always going to be top of the list. I even got a Hewes Crab tattoo this year on my arm."[45]

Despite working with many of the noted varieties, Taylor has also developed an affection for an old English bittersweet variety, the Yarlington Mill, which was first discovered in 1898 in Somerset. The first time Taylor made a small batch with Yarlington Mill, there was a distinct leather flavor in the cider, which he described as "like biting your couch."[46] He wasn't sure what he thought about it. When Courtney tried it, though, it brought a tear to her eye, as she had long wanted that West Country character in the Blue Bee ciders. In future batches, Taylor blended in some Tremlett's Bitter and Bramley's Seedling to diffuse the leather character while keeping the rich, indulgent nature of the finest West Country scrumpy ciders.

While Blue Bee is primarily known for single varietal ciders featuring the classic Virginian apples, such as Hewes Crab and Harrison, they also produce a range called Orchard Potluck that is more of a collaboration between Blue Bee and their supplier orchards. Each year, they work with the orchards to learn what apples the orchardists are particularly excited about that harvest and then experiment with various yeast strains and blends to make about five batches per year.

Taylor and Mackenzie also, while deeply informed by the classic cider world, don't feel the need to stick strictly within the limits of its traditions and do make ciders mixed with other fruits, such as Petit Manseng grapes, or aged in whiskey barrels from Catoctin Creek Distillery.

In early 2024, Taylor and Mackenzie completed the move of Blue Bee's cidery and tasting room to Bethlehem Road. Open Wednesday through Sunday, it's a beautiful, spacious place where love of cider shines through.

BLUE TOAD HARD CIDER

Roseland, Nelson County

Blue Toad was established by childhood friends Todd Rath, Scott Hallock and Greg Booth in 2015, though its origins lie in 2013, when the friends would experiment with making hard ciders, mostly using varieties like Granny Smith, Red Delicious and Golden Delicious from local orchards. Another of the cideries on the well-worn destination for craft drinkers that is Route 151, Blue Toad Cider is located on a historic twenty-seven-acre farm, surrounded by the wooded hills of the Virginia Piedmont, with the South Fork Rockfish River coursing its way through the property.

At the heart of the Blue Toad Cider Farm is the Cider Hall, a tasting room and event space, which has idyllic views of the aforementioned hills surrounding the farm, views that can be taken in from the outside seating on the meadow and patio.

All the cider fermentation happens in the Cider Hall, right behind the tasting room, while the apples themselves are sourced from orchards in Nelson County. When it comes to their ciders, the team at Blue Toad focuses on drinkability and balance: neither sweet nor fully dry and with an abv of around 5 percent. Blue Toad's flagship cider is its Blue Ridge Blonde, made with locally sourced Golden and Red Delicious apples, as well as Granny Smith.

This modern approach extends to those ciders Blue Toad flavors with other ingredients, such as black cherry, raspberry and cranberries, as well as traditional holiday spices during the winter months. Blue Toad also produces a seasonal cider specifically for St Patrick's Day, Paddy Green, made from 100 percent Granny Smith apples grown in the Blue Ridge Mountains.

BOLD ROCK HARD CIDER

Nellysford, Nelson County

In 2010, John Washburn had a vision: to create a modern cider company that would tap into the growing public consciousness that cider was more than just freshly pressed apple juice. He teamed up with New Zealander Brian Shanks, a world-renowned expert in cider, and Bold Rock Cider in Nelson County was born.

Right at the heart of busy Route 151, Bold Rock Cider boasts one of the busiest tasting rooms on the trail.

Taking advantage of property owned by John, Bold Rock was the first cidery established on the popular Route 151, located between Afton's Blue Mountain Brewery and the original Devils Backbone Basecamp in Roseland. In 2011, John and Brian built the first cider barn on the property, and the following year saw the first batch of Bold Rock Cider hit the market. That initial batch was a fermentation of locally sourced Granny Smith apples, which resulted in a refreshing, easy-drinking, session-strength cider.

In its first year of production, Bold Rock far exceeded initial expectations, selling sixfold more cider than projected. Clearly, it had found a niche in Virginia's cider-loving community, and it has continued to grow in the years since. In 2014, John and Brian fulfilled their original vision of opening a cider-focused brewpub on one of the most popular craft alcohol routes in Virginia. The new barn, affectionately referred to as the Chapel of Apple, features a beautiful taproom, built with reclaimed oak beams, and a patio with one of the finest views of the Rockfish valley.

The original cider barn is now home to the Bold Rock Barrel Barn, converted in 2017, where the cider makers produce smaller, experimental batches of cider, often fermenting or aging the results in wooden barrels.

The Barrel Barn has been kitted out with a cozy tasting room. In addition to its original location in Nelson County, Bold Rock also has a tasting room at the Carter Mountain Orchards close to Charlottesville, which boasts magnificent views over rural Central Virginia.

The majority of Bold Rock's ciders are very definitely in the modern style, featuring additional fruit flavors such as blackberry, pineapple and hops in a cider called India Pressed Apple, riffing off the beer phenomenon that is IPA. The Granny Smith cider is still available, and Bold Rock now also produces a stronger cider called Imperial Cider, again borrowing a term from beer brewing. In addition to its core range of fruit-flavored ciders, Bold Rock also produces a range of limited edition ciders that are only available at the taproom in Nelson County.

In late 2019, Bold Rock joined Artisanal Brewing Ventures, dramatically increasing its reach throughout the Southeast and making it one of the best-selling cider brands in the region, while still supporting local orchards.

BRYANT'S CIDER

Farm and Cidery: Roseland, Nelson County
Tasting Room: Richmond

Jerry Thornton, owner and cider maker at Bryant's Cider, grew up regularly visiting his grandparents' farm in Nelson County, and when his grandmother passed away in 2016, it was left to him to take responsibility for the farm, known as Edgewood. Rather uniquely, Edgewood has remained in the same family since it was established in the 1860s.

Being in Nelson County, one of the main apple-growing regions in Virginia, Edgewood has long played host to an orchard: the original trees were planted in the immediate aftermath of the Civil War in 1865. That orchard would remain in place for more than one hundred years, until Hurricane Camille swept its way through Nelson County, torrenting more than twenty-five inches of rain on the land in a matter of five hours. The orchards at Edgewood and much of Nelson County's agricultural land did not survive the deluge, and it took many years of restoration to bring Edgewood back from this disaster.

As of 1998, Edgewood once again boasted an orchard, its forty-five acres planted with apple trees that are still there, though they are now leased to a local orchardist.

The Bryant's Cider taproom in the Scott's Addition district in Richmond is an avowedly bohemian spot to hang out.

In 2015, keenly aware of the continuing growth of traditional cider in Virginia, Jerry decided to investigate the possibility of growing cider apples on the farm, with the aim of making Edgewood a sustainable concern. Around the same time, he started trying locally produced ciders, such as those from Albemarle CiderWorks and Potter's Craft, admitting that the kind of ciders Potter's was producing suited his palate far more, especially compared to the exceedingly sugary ciders being put out by national brands catering to a mass market.

Working with the orchardist that leases part of Edgewood, Jerry started making cider—lots and lots of cider—working out his recipes and the flavors he wanted to showcase. He also set about planting another twelve acres of land with apple trees, this time focusing on traditional American cider varieties. Within a couple months of the cider orchard being planted, disaster struck again when all the trees died.

Undeterred, though also convinced that it would be better to work with the orchards already in Nelson County as a source for juice, Jerry attended the Cider Institute of North America and then the Craft Beer Program at the University of Richmond in order to learn what he needed to run a craft cider business. The outcome was Bryant's Cider, which started production in January 2018.[47]

At Edgewood, Jerry converted the original farmhouse into a cidery and production center, as the infrastructure was already in place, and then opened a tasting room on the estate in the latter months of 2018, with a focus on classic dry ciders. Aware that getting to the farm in Nelson County, located deep in Virginia's beautiful Piedmont region and on the popular Route 151, can be something of a trek for many people, Jerry decided to open a remote tasting room in Richmond, initially in Jackson Ward. It moved to Shockoe Bottom in 2020, just as the COVID-19 pandemic was beginning and as Bryant's was becoming a viable business. When the pandemic ended, the passing foot traffic that urban tasting rooms are heavily reliant on didn't return to the Shockoe Bottom location, so they found themselves on the move again, this time to Richmond's bohemian district, Carytown.

The Carytown tasting room is very much in keeping with the district's bohemian vibe and reminds me of many of the artsy pubs and bars I frequented when I lived in Prague.

When it comes to his cider, Jerry is passionate about forging his own path rather than doing what everyone else is up to. As such, he aims to be as creative as possible, while working with apples that come strictly from Nelson County. To add layers of flavor on top of the dry character of his cider, Jerry adds ingredients such as pumpkin spice, hibiscus and even a rosemary/cranberry combination, for his winter seasonal cider.

Aware that many cider drinkers are looking for a sweeter expression of the apple, Jerry has also launched Bryant's Basic, a line of slightly sweeter and modern, flavored, styles of cider, with an abv topping out at 5 percent.

Jerry is always looking for a unique spin for his Bryant's Ciders, though he believes strongly in not using concentrates or artificial flavorings; to that end, everything that goes into his cider is freshly pressed or picked ahead of use.

BUSKEY CIDER

Richmond

The year was 2012, and Buskey Cider founder Will Correll found himself on the horns of a dilemma: he had fallen in love with the history of American cider but was distinctly disappointed with the cider choices at the store. In order to rectify the situation, he did what many cider makers have done down the years: started making his own, while still a student at the historic Hampden-Sydney College.

The next few years were spent learning everything he could about cider, including how to make the ciders he was fermenting everything he believed they could be, and in 2015, he decided to make the leap from home brewer to professional cider maker. Will spent that year looking for a location for his cidery in the up-and-coming Scott's Addition district of Richmond, which had seen several craft breweries move into the neighborhood—and so, given Will's modern approach to cider, it seemed like the ideal location. Will's new cidery would be housed in a warehouse that had once been used for loading the railroad cars that trundled through Richmond.

When it came to a name for his new cidery, Will harked back to colonial times, when cider was the number one drink, with the word *buskey*, recorded for history by perhaps the greatest raconteur and bon vivant of the Founding

Serving pitchers at Buskey Cider in Richmond.

Fathers, Benjamin Franklin. Franklin penned a list of synonyms for drunkenness titled "The Drinkers Dictionary," which was published under his pseudonym Poor Richard in the *Pennsylvania Gazette* in 1737.[48]

In the spring of 2016, Buskey Cider opened its doors, making ciders from 100 percent Virginia-grown apples sourced from various orchards around the state. In recent years, Buskey has started working with Silver Creek and Seaman's Orchards to get the juice it needs. In 2023, Allen Crump came on board as the head cider maker. Once a regular at the Buskey tasting room in Scott's Addition, Allen worked in the tasting room bar before moving over to making cider. While Allen is the head cider maker, Will is still involved in the production side of the cidery.

In describing Buskey's philosophy of cider making, Allen notes that it is "a combination of two opposing forces, the rich history and culture—in Virginia in particular—of cider, and we want to incorporate and honor that and, being in the middle of Scott's Addition, challenging the notions of what flavors could be."[49]

The goal for Allen in bringing together the "opposing forces" of tradition and modernity is to attract new audiences to cider, in much the same way as he was drawn into the cider world, having come from a beer-drinking background: "I came from beer, where they were doing all these crazy things, and I came in here and there was an Earl Grey Lemon Ginger cider on tap, and it was really wonderful."[50] Before this, the cider Allen knew was the big national brands that can be found on the supermarket shelves wherever you go, so it was an eye-opener for him that cider could be so different.

While Buskey does make lots of ciders with different, interesting flavors, the heart of the cidery is still those ciders that are all about the apples themselves. Its flagship cider, Buskey Dry, is a classic bone-dry cider that is also crushingly refreshing. Buskey also pays homage to the older traditions of Virginia cider with its Heritage Blend, which takes a recently discovered crab apple from a seedling tree and the classic Ashmead's Kernel and modern GoldRush apples to craft a slightly sweeter, though still delightfully dry, cider.

Although there are a handful of apple trees growing outside the tasting room, it is clear that they're not enough to feed the stainless steel fermentation tanks inside the cidery. Buskey is very open about working with Silver Creek Orchards to source the apples that go into its ciders. Allen describes the relationship with Silver Creek as "invaluable for us. It allows us to really specialize. They grow great apples, we make great cider, and we have an open line of communication so we can find out about what is good in the orchard in any given year."[51]

Vintage cider press outside the Halcyon Days Cider tasting room, Natural Bridge.

The Troddenvale at Oakley Farm orchard features apple trees from Spain, France and England as well as the United States.

A selection of picked apples in a basket at Albemarle CiderWorks.

A glass of Potter's Craft Cider on their patio in Albemarle County.

Big Fish Cider has won many awards, including a gold medal at the 2023 Virginia Governor's Cup for its outstanding Northern Spy single varietal.

Staunton's Ciders from Mars produces a wide range of superb ciders, many of which have won prestigious awards.

Reflected glory: Lost Boy Cider's Comeback Kid at the artistic tasting room in Alexandria's Old Town.

"Drink cider," says this poster at Courthouse Creek Cider in Goochland County. We heartily agree.

Rustic fencing and verdant fields at the Widow's Watch orchard, in Edinburg, Shenandoah County, reflect the most common context for Virginia apple growing.

Orchard post markers at Widow's Watch Cider.

An autumnal glass of Back Bay's graff in the tasting room garden.

High-density orcharding at Tumbling Creek Cider in Meadowview, Washington County.

Bottles of Sage Bird's Long Night pommeau ready to be bought and drunk.

Cider by the fire at Mt. Defiance Cider Barn, Loudoun County, as autumn weather draws in.

Tree trunks repurposed for high-density orcharding at Troddenvale at Oakley Farm.

A glass of cider in front of the press in the cozy Cobbler Mountain Cellars tasting room.

The orchards at Albemarle CiderWorks as the leaves turn in the Virginia Piedmont.

The lively, vibrant Sage Bird tasting room in Harrisonburg is the ideal setting for their flavorful ciders.

The Chartres Cathedral maze–inspired orchards at Halcyon Days Cider.

The new and the old: a stainless steel hydraulic press and the classic homestead screw press.

A mountain orchard in Highland County, laid out by legendary orchardist Tom Burford and now providing apples for Big Fish Cider.

From barrel to glass: Charlottesville's Patois Ciders undergo secondary fermentation in the bottle, just like sparkling wines, including disgorgement to remove dead yeast from the bottle.

Ancient-style agricultural tools are scattered around the Henway Hard Cider tasting room in Bluemont.

Troddenvale believes in interfering with the natural processes of an orchard as little as possible; it is one of the most serene places we visited.

The orchard at Courthouse Creek Cider in Goochland County supplies by far the majority of co-owner Eric's apples for his cider.

Cider, a drink born of agriculture, meets industrial design at the Wild Hare Cider tasting room in Berryville.

Potter's Craft Cider Farmhouse Dry on a solid wooden table in their converted chapel tasting room.

Buskey Cider's award-winning ciders are available in their Scott's Addition tasting room, including their Virginia Hewes Crab gold medal winner.

That free and open communication with Silver Creek orchard led to Buskey using the Ruby Red Crab Apple as part of its Heritage Blend, which won a Gold Medal at GLINTCAP 2023, as well as in a single varietal that won Best in Show Cider at the Virginia Governor's Cup in 2024.

As is so common a theme within the Virginia cider world, the cider makers at Buskey are fully aware, and respectful, of the depth of history that cider has, yet they refuse to be hidebound to that history as they create ciders that are modern, innovative and interesting. Most important of all, they are creating ciders that deserve to find an audience of traditionalists looking for expressions purely of the apple as much as those seeking a diversity of flavors and experiences.

CASTLE HILL CIDER

Keswick, Albemarle County

If any of the cideries in Virginia is emblematic of the history of apples and their fortunes, it is surely Castle Hill, which occupies about half of the 1,200-acre Castle Hill estate, which can trace its origins to a pre–Revolutionary

War land grant. The founder of the estate was an eminent physician, planter, explorer and friend to many in Virginia's high society of the day: Dr. Thomas Walker.

According to tradition, Dr. Walker, on his return from the Battle of Brandywine in 1777, brought with him scions of the Newtown Pippin apple variety. One of the oldest American varieties, the Newtown Pippin traces its origins to Long Island as a seedling variety, which was so well regarded it was introduced to England from America in the 1750s. As a result of Dr. Walker's scions, it would come to be known in Virginia as the Albemarle Pippin, a variety beloved of Jefferson, Washington and many others at the time. The original Albemarle Pippin trees from Dr. Walker's scions are long since gone, however.

The modern Castle Hill Cider was established in 2010, with the express intention to create cider that embodies the "pervading spirit of a place," a place that boasts about five thousand apple trees in its orchard.[52] As well as Albemarle Pippin, the orchards are home to renowned cider varieties such as Harrison, Virginia Hewes Crab and Esopus Spitzenberg, as well as more than twenty others. In pursuit of capturing the essence of place, Castle Hill's ciders very much lean toward the more traditional, and drier, style as being the fullest expression of the apples themselves.

The majority of the ciders produced at Castle Hill are crafted using multiple apple varieties to create distinct blends—rather than single varietals, as you will find at many other cideries. The heart of most Castle Hill blends is the Albemarle Pippin, as well as the modern Harrison variety. The cidery has two flagship ciders, Serendipity and Levity, both of which are multiple award winners. Serendipity is described as a "Goldilocks" cider, in that it is not too sweet yet not too dry; it was the first cider to win a gold medal at the Governor's Cup, in 2017.

Levity, Castle Hill's second flagship, is perhaps one of the most unique ciders being made in the United States, let alone Virginia. Like the other ciders produced at Castle Hill, it is a blend, and it is a dry cider; however, unlike the others, it is a marriage of intercontinental traditions, inspired by the owner and the cider maker's chance encounter with Georgian wine while in Italy. So impressed were they by the character of Georgian wine that they wanted to re-create something similar in the cider world, so they buried eight *qvevri* (pronounced "kway-vree") in the grounds of the cidery.

Qvevri are egg-shaped fermentation vessels made of terra-cotta that find their historic roots in the amphorae of the ancient world; there is evidence of qvevri being used to make wine in Georgia going back to around 6000

The award-winning Castle Hill Cider in Albemarle County has one of the most elegant tasting rooms in Virginia.

BCE.[53] Each vessel is lined with beeswax, produced by Castle Hill's own bees, on the inside and buried in the ground up to its neck. The fermentation is entirely wild, meaning that the cider maker doesn't add any yeast to the vessel, using only that which naturally occurs in the freshly pressed apple juice itself. Submerged in the red clay of Virginia, the qvevri are temperature controlled by the geothermal properties of the soil. The shape of the vessels encourages the yeast and must to circulate and, as fermentation completes, to clarify entirely naturally. Once fermented, the cider is left in the qvevri to mature until the cider maker decides it is ready to be packaged. Fermenting in earthenware vessels with just the natural yeast of the apples results in a bone-dry cider that sparkles with spicy notes backing up the funkiness of wild fermentation.

Continuing the transcontinental theme, Castle Hill also created a unique bar experience harking back to what is considered by many in the Virginia cider world to be the spiritual home of the drink: England. For British people of a certain age, and army brats like myself, the Land Rover Defender is simply an iconic vehicle. The Defender comes in two wheelbases, the shorter 90 and the longer 110. It's one of the former that Castle Hill converted into its mobile bar, the Landy Bar, from which visitors to the cidery in Keswick are able to purchase bottles to enjoy on the Castle Hill grounds.

Not only is Castle Hill Cider one of the finest cider makers in Virginia, but the cidery itself is also as beautiful a place to sit and enjoy the nectar of nature as could possibly be imagined. Set in the rolling foothills of the Virginia Piedmont, just off Route 231 between Charlottesville and Gordonsville, it is a place of tranquility in equal measure to Levity and Serendipity. As of April 2024, the tasting room at Castle Hill Cider is open only for reservations of more than ten people, though it will also open to the public occasionally for bottle sales.

CIDER LAB

Sumerduck, Fauquier County

Cider Lab is one of the most eclectic and broad-ranging cider makers in Virginia today. It was established in 2020, right at the height of the COVID-19 pandemic. Father-and-son team A.J. and James Rasure combine full-time careers elsewhere with making a range of flavored ciders, perries and "jerk'ms"—drinks made from pitted fruits such as apricots and peaches, then fermented in the same manner as cider—as a side hustle.

The Rasures consider themselves "cider scientists," and their experiments with fermented beverages started with a glut of tomatoes from James's garden and the long-held notion that it is possible to turn basically anything into wine. The resultant tomato wine didn't live up to expectations, and so father A.J. bought his son a winemaking class in nearby Fredericksburg.

As they learned how to make wine, a friend asked them to make some cider but opted against purchasing the six gallons they had made. In the spirit of home brewers everywhere, they added habanero to the mix, followed by some maple syrup, as they felt the spice was overbearing in the original batch. They were so encouraged by the result that they took some to a local brewery to get feedback. The brewery promptly started buying five gallons a week to sell through its taproom, and thus Cider Lab was born.

Eventually, the Rasures would open their own taproom in Fauquier County with their flagship Mango Habanero Cider, as well as other potions like Blackberry Hibiscus Cider and Sumerduck Cider, in which a wine of blueberries, blackberries and raspberries is blended with the base cider. The team also create perries, pear-based drinks, such as the pie-inspired Strawberry Rhubarb Perry.

Above: Ceramic growlers are available at Cider Lab to take their ciders away with you.

Right: An antique wooden cider press sits outside the Cider Lab cidery and tasting room in Sumerduck, Fauquier County.

The original taproom, located on Route 651 in Sumerduck, offers ciders on tap, as well as outside seating for enjoying the location and a food truck, though it is only open Wednesday through Sunday. In addition to the original taproom, Cider Lab also has a second location in Spotsylvania Courthouse, which is open seven days a week and has food options available.

CIDERS FROM MARS

Staunton

Located in the heart of the city of Staunton, Ciders from Mars opened the doors to its taproom in 2021, though the initial spark of inspiration came in 2017, during that year's solar eclipse. As is a common theme among the current generation of cider makers in Virginia, Ciders from Mars founders Nikki West and Jeremy Wimpey had gained experience in cider making by volunteering at a friend's cidery and fermenting their own ciders at home. In creating their cidery, Nikki and Jeremy have forged together their scientific and artistic backgrounds to produce something distinctive, quirky and deeply fun.

As well as having a taproom, Ciders from Mars's Staunton location is home to a production laboratory, where Nikki takes her scientific training—prior to the cidery, she was a geochemist—and creates the various blends and flavored ciders that the cidery is well known for. Ciders from Mars does have a small orchard focused on traditional cider apples in the western part of Augusta County, but it is not open to the public.

In terms of the ciders themselves, Ciders from Mars skillfully weaves together traditional and modern influences to produce a range of ciders, particularly its flagship cider, Hellas Dry. Combining traditional American cider apple varieties with more modern apples, all of which are grown in Virginia, Hellas Dry is a clean, dry cider with citrus and tropical fruit flavors, accentuated by a crisp mineral character.

Ciders from Mars also produces single varietal ciders with several of the classic apples so synonymous with Virginia, such as the Hewes Crab (called Hues), Harrison (called Shady Lady) and Winesap (called Hazy Lady). Given Nikki and Jeremy's willingness to experiment with process and ingredients, Ciders from Mars is one of the few Virginia cideries that puts some of its products in bourbon barrels to age: its DeStijl is aged in former Kentucky bourbon barrels for four months before being bottled.

In the heart of Staunton, Ciders from Mars straddles classic and modern cider making with scientific precision and ineffable ease.

At the heart of the operation is the taproom in downtown Staunton, where self-selected tasting flights are available, as are draught cider by the glass and bottles to take home. Whether sitting inside, where you can view the production lab with its collection of stainless steel vessels and measuring instruments, or on the deck overlooking the Wharf Area Historical District, the vibe at Ciders from Mars is relaxed and welcoming.

COBBLER MOUNTAIN CIDER

Delaplane, Fauquier County

Set on ninety acres of wooded hillside, Cobbler Mountain Cider is the fulfillment of several dreams. When Laura McCarthy Louden's father bought the land on which the cidery is set in the 1950s, it was his dream that it become a family farm. It was only in the early years of the twenty-first century, though, with the land having lain largely barren since her father's early death, that Laura and her husband, Jeff—now co-owners of Cobbler Mountain—realized they shared his dream.

Deep in rural Loudoun County, in the shadow of the eponymous mountain, Cobbler Mountain Cellars' ciders are inspired by the owners' West Country ancestry.

Jeff had been making wine and cider at home for several years, and the realization that Laura's father had longed to build a productive family farm was enough to entice Jeff and Laura back to Virginia, where they started the task of restoring the land to productivity and realizing their dream of running a cidery. Having cleared the land, planted trees, cut trails through the woods and built a new road on the property, they opened their doors in the summer of 2011, initially selling a combination of wine and cider, though they have focused in recent years purely on cider.

As with many other cideries, the heartbeat of Cobbler Mountain is the beautifully restored barn that operates as both production space and taproom, with a selection of eight draught ciders, as well as a range of bottled ciders. There is also plenty of outside space, with picnic tables, to enjoy the magnificent views of the mountains that give the cidery its name.

With family roots in the West Country of England, Cobbler Mountain's ciders naturally lean toward the English pub cider tradition, with alcohol levels rarely exceeding 7 percent. Despite Jeff and Laura's preference for the West Country tradition, Cobbler Mountain ciders also incorporate a plethora of fruit, spices and other ingredients, including honey, watermelon and ginger, making their offerings much more in the modern vein.

The Present

CORCORAN VINEYARDS & CIDER

Waterford, Loudoun County

When Lori and Jim Corcoran started Corcoran Vineyards in 2004, it was a pure winery, making only traditional grape-based wines at the Corcorans' property near Waterford, Loudoun County. In 2011, they decided to expand into brewing beer as well, though in a different location, while remaining on the family property. When they decided to set up a distinct location for the brewery in 2013, in nearby Purcellville, Lori was already making an apple wine as part of her offering, using apples from local orchards in Northern Virginia.

Unlike others making apple wine in Virginia at the time, Lori's approach was to allow the yeast to ferment completely out, making a dry wine rather than taking the well-worn path of sweeter products. While the brewery was no longer on the property, customers at Corcoran wanted to have some kind of carbonated beverage, and as Lori herself says: "The gluten-free alternative to beer is cider, and so I opted to get a couple more pieces of equipment and instead of making apple wine, make it into cider."[54]

Despite Lori's wine-making background, Corcoran's ciders are lower in alcohol than a standard wine, with Lori aiming for an abv of around 7 percent and then carbonating the cider to give it that effervescence her customers were looking for. As Corcoran is located in a part of Virginia that has plenty of small, boutique wineries, adding cider to her product range was a way for Lori to stand out from the crowd at a time when cider's star was still in the early stages of its rise.

Having become friends with Brian Shanks of Bold Rock Cider, before releasing her first cider to the world, Lori took some down to Nelson County to get his opinion. On seeing Brian react to her cider with a big smile on his face, Lori realized, "OK, so I did a good job."[55]

Given the following her ciders have garnered, Lori has focused on the cider side of her fermentation, and therefore, the only wine she still makes is a port wine that she ages for eight years in whiskey barrels.

Describing her approach to cider making, Lori comments that she makes the kind of ciders she herself would want to drink, a throwback to when she first made the apple wine and her husband asked, "Will people buy it?"—to which Lori responded, "Well, I like it." It is this philosophy that has guided her cider making ever since. "I don't like things to be sugary sweet," she says. "I like them naturally sweet."[56]

Left: Corcoran Vineyards and Cider is located in one of the most historic districts in the nation.

Below: The Corcoran Hard Cider, a sweeter cider, is fermented with champagne yeast for a crisp finish.

The Corcoran Vineyards & Cider tasting room is located somewhat off the beaten track, along very rural roads, in a barn that originally dates from the eighteenth century, from which Lori and Jim serve five different types of cider. Their flagship is the Corcoran Hard Cider, which, in keeping with Lori's preference, is fermented completely dry; she uses champagne yeast to allow the apple flavors and aromas to shine without being overshadowed by the yeast. Not every cider Lori makes uses the champagne yeast, as she also uses a specific cider strain, as well as using both yeasts from time to time, to highlight different characteristics of the cider.

As a subtle twist on its original hard cider, Corcoran also makes a version where the must is allowed to sit on apple skins and extract a subtle rosé color and a touch of tannins, adding to the mouthfeel. They also have a selection of flavored ciders, featuring peach and cinnamon, as well as one that is aged in bourbon barrels.

COURTHOUSE CREEK CIDER

Maidens, Goochland County

In 2013, Eric and Liza of Courthouse Creek Cider decided to up sticks from the Central Coast of California and its wine-centric universe and relocate to central Virginia. Prior to moving to Virginia, Eric was a private chef who also practiced law, while Liza was a schoolteacher, and both of them were avid fans of the wine culture in the area around Paso Robles and Templeton. Coming from such a strong wine-growing region, they originally thought that they would be planting grapes and starting a vineyard when they landed in Virginia with their blended family of kids from previous relationships.

That original plan to start their own wine-focused business came to a screeching halt when, on a whim, they dropped into Albemarle CiderWorks to do a tasting and a light bulb went off. Like several other cider makers in Virginia, they attended seminars that the Sheltons put on, and as Eric says: "At the time, there were maybe 250 to 300 wineries in Virginia and maybe 9 or 10 cideries. We were one of maybe 10 other people in the room interested in opening a cidery, and we thought, *See, there's a market here, and why not get in on something that's starting?*"[57]

Reflecting on the realization that they wanted to move in the direction of growing apples for cider, they came to the conclusion that they wanted to be an estate cidery. Such an approach to cider fit nicely into their overarching philosophy that they call "culterra," which Eric clarifies as "the fusion of culture and terra. The idea is: it is of the people and of the land. It's our interpretation of terroir and a sense of place."[58]

The ten acres of land that they eventually purchased with a view to setting up their estate cidery was completely empty when they bought it, and rather than charging headlong into planting trees, they prepared the land through cover cropping and doing soil analyses to learn what they needed to do to develop the soils before ever putting a tree in the ground.

Given Eric's experience with the wine-making community in California, he already had a solid grasp of the basics of fermentation. While getting the land ready, he also attended Cornell's Cider Institute of North America. With that formal training complete, Eric started making cider in his garage and learning the intricacies of cider fermentation and, as he admits, "fell hook, line and sinker for the cider revival that was afoot in the States."[59]

Inspired by a cidery in Maryland that had adopted many of the practices of the natural wine movement, Courthouse Creek opened its doors in 2014 as the first natural cider maker in Virginia. While Eric was headed down the rabbit hole of making cider, Liza was in the orchard growing the fruit with an eye to being all-natural and organic, eschewing the use of pesticides or sprays, given that the ten-acre lot, as well as being their dream agri-business, was also their home.

As well as being committed to producing natural cider, Courthouse Creek has also fermented in barrels from the beginning, which Eric admits was partially a cost-saving effort: used barrels from local wineries were cheaper than stainless steel fermenting vessels, as well as being easier to fit in their two-car garage.

However, the driving force in all their decisions is being true to themselves and not just being in cider to make money. In summing up their philosophy, Eric says, "We really feel that if you know why you want to do it, and that's a deeper interest than just making a buck and it's really tied to who you are as an individual, then it's so much easier to sell, as you are being very true: it comes from the heart."[60]

In many ways, Eric and Liza wanted to re-create an element of the wine culture they had known in California before it became hugely popular, in that they wanted people to be able to interact with them directly, as they had done with winemakers whose hands were stained purple with juice.

While waiting for their orchard to produce the fruit they needed for their ciders, Eric and Liza sourced apples from large commercial orchards within Virginia, as well as from Henley's Orchard near Charlottesville, from whom

In the depths of rural Goochland County, Courthouse Creek Cider advocates making natural cider, with all the risks that entails.

they bought the Black Twig that made their first single varietal. Since their orchard has matured and is producing fruit, Courthouse Creek cider is now made with just their own apples, which inevitably means that the production is small and will remain so.

In their orchard, Eric and Liza grow twenty-four apple varieties, including Parmar, Black Twig, Father Abraham's and GoldRush, as well as several English and French cider apple varieties. The orchard sits right opposite their tasting room, which is the only place that Courthouse Creek Cider is available from, as they have no ambition to join the distribution rat race, preferring to focus on that personal connection with folks who make the drive to Goochland County.

Although their approach to both their orchard and cider making is to be all natural, that doesn't mean the ciders they are producing are pure 100 percent apple ferments. They do use other fruits, such as raspberries and blackberries, as well as hops, all of which are grown on the farm, to infuse additional flavors, though the apples are always the star of the show.

COYOTE HOLE CRAFT BEVERAGES

Mineral, Louisa County

Coyote Hole Craft Beverages, originally Coyote Hole Ciderworks, was established in the Lake Anna area of Louisa County in 2015 by husband-and-wife duo Chris and Laura Denkers. In the years before taking the plunge to open a cidery, the Denkers were active home brewers, making beer, wine and cider to share with their friends and family. Eventually, they listened to the advice of those friends and family members who encouraged them that there was a market for the modern ciders they were producing.

Situated on more than thirty-five acres of wooded land, the Coyote Hole taproom and production facility has a bar serving both ciders and, as of 2023, beer as well. The tasting room itself has the classic rustic feel of many a cider barn, with plenty of outside (though under cover) seating.

All the apples used in Coyote Hole's range of ciders are sourced from the orchards of the Blue Ridge Mountains, and when using other ingredients, the Denkers make a point of sourcing them from local farmers and producers when possible. Their flagship cider, and one of the earliest ciders that Coyote Hole produced, is Oma Smith's, described as a "green apple hard cider"

Apples on tap at the Coyote Hole Craft Beverages taproom in Mineral, Louisa County.

that is made with a blend of three varieties of green apples; Granny Smith apple juice is then added at packaging to create a medium-sweet cider.

The cider range at Coyote Hole falls firmly within the modern vein, with several regular ciders featuring other flavorings such as orange, mango—and even cabernet franc and white wine, in their sangria-inspired ciders. Coyote Hole produces seasonal ciders imbued with the flavors of their respective times of year, such as Apparition, a pumpkin-infused cider available in the fall.

DARING CIDER AND WINE CO.

Patrick County

In 1970, Jocelyn Kuzelka's parents managed to escape from the euphemistically labeled "normalization" inflicted on the people of what was then Czechoslovakia as part of the brutal suppression of the Prague Spring. Eventually they found their way to Virginia and started a farm in Patrick County, deep in Southwest Virginia. It was here that Jocelyn would grow up and eventually start her cider- and wine-making business.

Having studied biochemistry at university and looking for something fun to do for a few months between graduating and starting a career, Jocelyn attended a wine festival, and given her academic background, she realized that the confluence of wine and science was where she wanted to build her life's work. She got a job working for a small winery that gave her the opportunity to tour many of the wine-producing regions of the world, tasting wine and instilling within herself an appreciation of the relationship between wine and food.

As a result, Jocelyn decided that she wanted to be a winemaker, so she enrolled in a wine-making master's program in Australia, where she spent three years learning the necessary technical skills to make wine but also honing her sensory skills in order to describe the aromas and flavors being made and also to pinpoint flaws in wine and identify where they came from.

At the end of her time in Australia, Jocelyn headed back to Virginia and the family farm, which she took over in 2008 when her father passed away. Armed with the necessary skills, Jocelyn started a consultancy company, Panacea Wine Consulting, to help wine and cider makers to achieve their fullest potential. Her first client was Diane Flynt of Foggy Ridge Cider in neighboring Carroll County, where her remit was largely focused on product development. In 2010, Jocelyn took over production at Foggy Ridge, while Diane focused on sales and spreading the word about traditional cider.

It was around this time that Jocelyn would have a cider epiphany that, to this day, informs her cider-making philosophy: drinking the first batch of Albemarle CiderWorks' Virginia Hewes Crab single varietal and discovering that the acidic nature of crab apples suited her palate to a T.

Jocelyn maintained her role as cider maker until 2017, when Foggy Ridge decided to focus on apple growing rather than cider, all the while also consulting for several other Virginia cider makers, such as Castle Hill Cider in Albemarle County and Richmond's Blue Bee Ciderworks. Even with all her consulting work, Jocelyn was keenly aware of the fact that what she really wanted to do was to make her own products, and so Daring Cider and Wine Co. was born in 2021, in partnership with Jocelyn's best friend, Megan Hereford.

Although Jocelyn's preference leans more toward traditional, mostly American-style ciders, her process is deeply thoughtful, reflective of her sensory skills in designing the kind of cider she believes people will want to drink. She is as thoughtful in her yeast selection as she is in every part of the cider-making process; as she comments: "If we can choose the apples, why not also choose the yeast?"[61]

Such a controlled approach to fermentation allows Jocelyn to achieve her aim with all her ciders—for them to be primarily about the fruit—with as few yeast esters and phenols as possible and avoiding the funkiness of fermentation reliant on the wild yeast naturally present in the apples.

Like several of the cider makers profiled in this book, Jocelyn has a small orchard where she grows a certain amount of apples for her ciders. As she's someone who wants to support local agriculture wherever possible, that orchard is for growing varieties that she cannot buy elsewhere in Virginia.

While batches are inherently small, Daring's is high-quality cider, yet Jocelyn aims to keep her products as affordable as possible. Currently, Daring makes a triumvirate of ciders: Crab Apple Cider, a blend of Virginia Hewes Crab and Red Ruby Crab; Cider Ancestral, a blend of Ashmead's Kernel, American crab apples and Harrison; and finally, Serious Blend, which pulls together Old Virginia Winesap, Harrison and Ashmead's Kernel.

Daring Cider and Wine Co. doesn't have an open-to-the-public tasting room, though the team can be found pouring their ciders at events throughout Virginia, and it is possible to visit the farm in Patrick County by appointment.

DITCHLEY CIDER WORKS

Northumberland County

Ditchley Cider Works, the brainchild of Cathy Calhoun and Paul Grosklags, is located on the historic Ditchley Plantation, which Cathy and Paul purchased in 2014. The origins of the plantation go back to the late seventeenth century, when Hancock Lee built the first manor house on the property, having inherited it from the progenitor of the Lee Family in Virginia, Richard "the Immigrant" Lee, who arrived from England in 1639.

In order to make Ditchley a sustainable estate, Cathy and Paul planted orchards soon after buying the property with a view to starting a small, family-run cidery. The orchards consist of about fifty different apple varieties and are the sole source of apples for the cider they make.

Ditchley Cider Works currently makes four ciders, all of which are blends of the apples coming out of its own orchards. The ciders are Simple, a blend of European cider apples fermented just with the yeast naturally occurring in the apples themselves; G-8, so named for a team member's aviation call sign and a blend of Wickson Crab and Black Twig; Rivah, a Sops of Wine and Virginia Hewes Crab blend that is also dry hopped with Australian hops; and finally, Blush, which brings together Geneva and Redfield Crab to create a rosé cider as a result of using red-fleshed apples.

Only open on weekends, Ditchley also has a cider brunch each Sunday, with reservations required through their website.

HALCYON DAYS CIDER

Natural Bridge, Rockbridge County

When it comes to getting to Halcyon Days Cidery, the metaphor almost writes itself. Whether coming from the north or the south, you have to leave the bedlam that is driving on Interstate 81 and wind a little ways into the country to find this place of simplicity and beauty. Such attention to detail is hardly a surprise given owner and cider maker Larry Krietemeyer's former profession as an architect. It was a desire for change and the opportunity to do something that would re-root him in the natural world that brought Larry and his wife to the gently undulating hills of Rockbridge County.[62]

While Larry was born and raised in Florida, his wife has roots in Virginia's farming communities farther down the Shenandoah Valley, though apples did not play a major part in that history. Initially, they envisioned a log cabin in the mountains rather than a small Piedmont farm as their escape from hectic modernity, but the draw of cider and its simplicity proved to be too much, and so in 2012, they started Halcyon Days, which, as the name suggests, harks back to a simpler time when most farms had at least a home orchard from which cider would be made.

The property they found in which to realize their ambition of doing something to keep the mind busy while practicing a relatively simple craft was a former dairy farm; indeed, the production facility was first housed in the old milking barn, which was itself the last of the original buildings on the site. Despite being so close to the traffic buzzing up and down I-81, they wanted to have a tasting room that would embody their love of the simplicity of the past, and so they lovingly moved, and restored, a log cabin that had stood in Rockbridge County since the 1860s.[63]

While the focus of Halcyon Days is very much on respecting the elder days and the ancestors who came before and worked the land, practicing an ancient craft, Larry's former life as an architect is also evident in their orchard. Unlike the vast majority of cidery orchards, Halcyon Days' is not a grid or even row after row of tall spindle trees reaching for the sky; rather, it is a 1.7-mile labyrinth composed of about 2,500 trees. The inner circle of trees are a variety of apple native to the mountains of central Asia and China from which the modern domesticated apple tree, *malus domestica*, was developed. Coming out from the central Asian core are the classic cider apple trees of the European traditions found in France, Spain and England. Farther out in the concentric rings of trees are American heirloom varieties, until finally, you reach the outer circles: modern American varieties. Modeled after the legendary labyrinth of Chartres Cathedral in France, which was laid down in the thirteenth century, the Halcyon Days labyrinth is a pomological walking tour to the very beginnings of mankind's love of the apple. Perched on a knoll in the landscape, it also bears a remarkable resemblance to the hill forts found scattered throughout the cider-making West Country of England.

When it comes to the cider itself, again, Halcyon Days finds its bedrock in the older heirloom cider varieties that are the very basis of Virginian cider, Harrison and Hewes Crab. Its flagships are single varietal iterations of each: Jubilance and Occam's Razor, respectively. All the apples that are pressed into Halcyon Days' ciders are grown in one of the cidery's three orchards.

Outside Halcyon Days Cider, a statue of the legendary Johnny Appleseed stands guard over their maze-inspired orchard of concentric rings.

While Larry's own preference leans toward dry ciders, reflecting, perhaps, the influence of Albemarle CiderWorks' Chuck Shelton, he appreciates that many people coming into the tasting room have not experienced "hard" cider before and find the bracing dryness of a fully complete ferment to be challenging on the palate, so he has ciders to suit both the first-timer and the more experienced palate.[64]

While harking back to simpler times, Larry and his family also acknowledge the more whimsical nature of the innocence implicit in such simplicity. As such, they allow themselves to have fun with their cider and experiment with the flavor expressions possible through their apple blends, though the apple is always the star—even above the larger-than-life statue of Johnny Appleseed that stands outside the tasting room.

HENWAY HARD CIDER

Bluemont, Loudoun County

The village of Bluemont sits on the eastern side of Snicker's Gap, the main pass through the Blue Ridge Mountains between Loudoun County in Northern Virginia and the Lower Shenandoah Valley. It is here, in the rolling hills, that the Zurschmeide family settled in the early 1990s with a vision: to bring an old, disheveled farm, known today as Great Country Farm, back to life, restoring the soil through regenerative practices, all the while imagining the mountain brimming with vines and orchards.

While the vineyard vision would be realized in 2007 with the establishment of Bluemont Vineyard, it would be 2019 before their orchard was ready to produce cider. In the meantime, the Zurschmeides opened one of the first farm breweries in Virginia, making use of the produce of the land.

Although the Zurschmeides are very much hands-on in their family farm and respective businesses, the cider maker is Scott Spelbring, who says that during his interview for a position in the winery, he was asked: "How do you feel about cider?" Having been a winemaker for many years, Scott was also a fan of cider as a result of having "some English friends growing up, who turned me on to cider at a very young age, and so I've always loved it, especially its refreshing nature."[65]

On the family's side, the impetus behind starting Henway Hard Cider was that they were producing a lot of apples in their orchard and needed something to do with them. While Scott had been brought into

"How much does a henway?" goes the question; the rooster might know the answer.

the family business as the principal winemaker of Bluemont Vineyards, he started to experiment with apples for cider, partly as a way to make use of apples abandoned on the orchard floor by visitors coming to the farm in order to pick their own fruit. It was this experimentation that led to Scott's cider epiphany as he realized: "Gosh, there are differences with apples just as there are with grapes."[66]

This experimentation and "playing" with the differences between apple varieties convinced Scott that there was potential for a cidery as part of the family business. As they planned for Henway Hard Cider, the question came up time and again: "Where do we sell this?"—allied with a desire to educate the public about what cider is and the nuances that are an inherent part of its nature. The answer was to build the Henway Hard Cider tasting room as a location distinct from the brewery and winery.

As Scott was learning more about cider, he attended courses at the Cider Institute of North America at Cornell, and while he acknowledges that there is a great deal of overlap between wine making and cider making, the subtle differences between the two were his main takeaways.

Coming from a wine background, Scott is deeply influenced by oenological practices when it comes to making cider: "It's very easy to take the quick route with cider, where you think, *OK, I've got to ferment something and then load it up with a whole bunch of other stuff or add a load of flavors.* I don't do that with my wine, and I try not to do that with my ciders."[67]

That doesn't mean Scott isn't using other ingredients in his ciders, whether by co-fermenting with other fruits from the family farms, aging in barrels or using grape skins in the fermentation to add body and structure. For Scott, though, those elements are still in service of the cider itself being dry and the apple the star of the show.

Having access to produce from across the family farm and taking advantage of the fact that cider making is a quicker process in many ways

A nineteenth-century mill and press in the tasting room at Henway Hard Cider in Bluemont.

than wine making, Scott is excited by his ability to experiment at a very small scale, even as little as a few kegs, to try new things and get customer feedback quickly through the tasting room.

Although the farm has access to a well-established orchard, Henway Hard Cider does buy apples from orchards in Northern Virginia, largely because the apples being grown on the farm are primarily culinary and dessert apples rather than cider-specific. From the farm itself, though, Scott is a fan of the Albemarle Pippin, explaining, "They have a little bit of everything, and they have acidity, which as a winemaker I really like. I like Arkansas Black quite a bit, because I like tannins."[68]

Although Henway has done several single varietals, Scott wants to get away from that and develop a "house blend" that will be the basis of their Brut cider. Even so, Scott, as a fan of cider's deep history in Virginia, has ambitions to make small-scale batches that share the history of Virginia's apples through the medium of cider, again with the aim of educating people.

At the tasting room itself, an expansive, barn-style building with some really cool antique agricultural and cider-making equipment dotted around, there are three main ciders always on tap and an ever-shifting cast of supporting characters as Scott experiments at a small scale. His flagship cider is called the Coop and is a semisweet, lightly sparkling blend that maintains a refreshingly crisp, fruit-forward character. The Brut, as the name suggests, is Henway's dry, effervescent cider with a delightful minerality in the finish. The third regular cider is a co-ferment of apples with strawberries from Great Country Farms, pressed alongside the apples themselves.

LOST BOY CIDER

Alexandria

Located just a few hundred yards from the Alexandria National Cemetery and African American Heritage Memorial Park in Old Town, Alexandria, Lost Boy Cider opened its doors in 2019, only to see the outbreak of the COVID-19 pandemic slam them shut eight months later. Eventually, as life returned to something approaching normality, Lost Boy reopened, and it continues to live up to its mission to be a unifying force that encourages people to "explore deeper, learn deeper, and chase our dreams."[69]

Founded by Tristan Wright, Lost Boy is the outcome of love at first taste on a trip to Ireland in 2010. Tristan and his wife had an encounter with

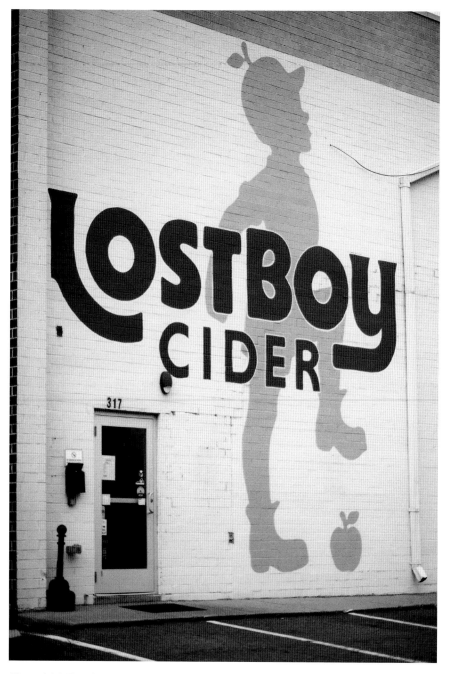

Alexandria's Lost Boy Cider, where honoring tradition and freedom to experiment go hand in hand.

A pint of Comeback Kid, Lost Boy's flagship dry cider.

a stag party—that's a bachelor party, for the uninitiated—that resulted in a night of singing and cider drinking. However, six years would pass before that brief Irish fling led to something more permanent. When he was diagnosed with a severe allergy to gluten and soy, Tristan knew that he needed to make drastic changes to his lifestyle, in particular regarding the alcohol he drank. Gone would be the whiskey and beer; in their place, eventually, came cider, naturally gluten free and thus not given to triggering his gluten allergy.

With vivid recollections of his experience with cider in Ireland, Tristan decided that he would become a cider maker; in particular, he wanted to "create an American-made, modern style, handcrafted cider." With the support of his family, he set about learning both how to make cider and run a cider business.

The cider that Tristan and his team make is rooted in the traditions of early Virginia cider makers yet looking to more modern horizons. Lost Boy's original flagship cider, appropriately called Comeback Kid, is a bone-dry cider made with apples from the Shenandoah Valley. To round out its core offering, Lost Boy also has ciders such as Wingman, with raspberries; En Fuego, featuring chili peppers; and Juicy, that uses hops as a nod to hazy IPAs. In 2021, just two years after opening its doors, Lost Boy was awarded Best in Show Cider at the prestigious Virginia Governor's Cup, the first year cider had its own category in the competition.

Drawing on Tristan and the team's passion for the traditions of Virginia cider, Lost Boy's Cellar Series is a collection of single varietal ciders starring the almost ubiquitous Harrison and Virginia Hewes Crab.

MT. DEFIANCE CIDER & DISTILLERY

Middleburg, Loudoun County

Established in 2014 by Marc Chretien, Mt. Defiance Cider has a singular aim in everything they do: to honor to the tradition of American cider making, using all Virginia-grown apples. Originally, the cidery and distillery

The Mt. Defiance Cider Barn is a spacious and elegant tasting room in which to enjoy their ciders.

coexisted in the same space in downtown Middleburg, but in 2017, Mt. Defiance built a custom-designed cider barn just a mile or so up the road.

Chretien has described the cider barn as "a fancy barn" that is spacious, at over eight thousand square feet, and has seating space for up to two hundred customers.[70] The barn itself sits on about twelve acres, on which an orchard has been planted with staples of the cider-making world, such as Grimes Golden and the ever popular Ashmead's Kernel. With plenty of seating on the barn patio as well and views over the surrounding countryside, Mt. Defiance is an oasis of calm on the edge of bustling Middleburg.

In terms of its ciders, Mt. Defiance straddles the line between the traditional Virginian dry ciders and more modern flavored ciders, as well as producing some single varietals. Their flagship Farmhouse Style Hard Cider is made with a blend of Virginia apples that finishes bone-dry; for an added kick, some of the flagship is further aged in bourbon barrels as General's Reserve Hard Cider. For something slightly more unique, Mt. Defiance ferments a cider with an English ale yeast strain, which produces the classic fruity characteristics of an English beer; the resulting cider, Old Volstead's, has a distinctly tangy flavor.

OLD HILL CIDERY

Timberville, Rockingham County

Old Hill Cidery is the cider-making operation of Showalter's Orchard, which was established in 1965 when current owner Shannon Showalter's father, Joe, purchased the orchard, though there has been an orchard on the property since the beginning of the twentieth century. The cidery itself was established in 2010 in order to take advantage of the upswing in interest in traditional cider.

Old Hill is one of a handful of cideries in Virginia that grows the vast majority of the apples they use in their products, with sixty acres of orchard on the farm growing some thirty varieties of apple. This "blossom to bottle" approach allows Old Hill to produce cider that is an expression of the land on which the orchard sits, at the top of a hill with stunning views into the Shenandoah Valley and the mountains on either side of the valley.

In 2019, with demand for their cider increasing, the Showalters decided to shut down their greenhouses on the farm and build a tasting room in order to have a place for visitors to come and experience their cider while soaking in the views. Old Hill is family owned and run: the cider maker is Shannon Showalter, who was born not long after his father started Showalter Orchards and is thus very much aware that cider apples need to be picked at just the right time in order to have the necessary sugar, acids and tannins that make great cider.

Most of the ciders that Shannon makes are firmly in the vein of the older, traditional approach to cider making in Virginia, with dry cider being the core of Old Hill's range. Given that the orchard supplies the majority of the apples being turned into cider, Shannon is able to make sure that Old Hill is pressing the right varieties together to meet the flavor profile he is looking for.

Emblematic of this traditional approach is Yesteryear, a dry cider using apple varieties that have stood the test of time and have their roots in the colonial period. In a nod to Shannon's childhood memories of people bringing their apples to be crushed and pressed and then taking the juice away with them in a barrel, Old Hill Cidermaker's Barrel is fermented in wooden barrels.[71] Being barrel fermented, as opposed to just barrel aged, the cider is reliant on the yeast naturally present in the juice, as well as yeasts and other bacteria that occur naturally in the wood of the barrel itself, which adds complexity to the eventual cider.

Although most of Shannon's ciders are traditional in style, he and his team regularly experiment with new approaches to cider, including creating some with additional fruits such as strawberry, peach and blackberry.

OLD TOWN CIDERY

Winchester

It is unlikely that there is a family name more associated with the apple-growing industry today than that of Glaize. It was in 1937 that Glaize Orchards spread through the Shenandoah Valley, and that business has stayed in the same family ever since, crossing four generations. It is perhaps, then, inevitable that when the current generation of Glaizes, Phillip and David, took on the family business, they would also find inspiration in the revival of traditional cider making in its one-time heartland. Thus, Old Town Cidery was born as one of the very few cider works in the state which is entirely "tree to can."[72]

Old Town Cidery's story begins in 2012, when generation four convinced generation three to grow cider apple varieties, grafting blocks of the classic Virginia Hewes Crab and a selection of classic English cider apples like Yarlington Mill and Bramley's Seedling—which, somewhat unusually for an apple used in cider, is a sharp, meaning it is high in acid but low in tannin. It was around this time that David started fermenting his own apple juice, experimenting with different blends and yeast strains and becoming deeply fascinated by the alchemy of fermentation.

Like many of the cider makers currently plying their trade in Virginia, David Glaize had "messed around with a bucket in the basement" prior to deciding to start a juice business and then a cidery.[73] He was fascinated most by the scientific underpinnings of fermentation and how yeast metabolized the sugar in the juice and ended up creating alcoholic cider. As well as the science, he was enamored, perhaps unsurprisingly, of the history of orchards and cider making in Virginia.

Phillip and David's original intention in growing cider apples was to sell them to cider makers, but increasingly, the cider makers wanted their juice ready pressed, which opened the idea to David of starting their own cidery; they hired cider maker Stephen Kelly in 2019. Starting their own cidery also gave the Glaizes the next step toward their orchard business and vertical integration that would make keeping their cider apple trees in the ground viable.[74]

When they decided to start Old Town Cidery, David looked to Chuck Shelton of Albemarle CiderWorks as a mentor, learning everything he could from the master. With heirloom apple varieties in place and Chuck Shelton as his mentor, David was convinced that he would be making classic Virginia-style dry ciders, mostly single varietals. Commercial reality soon took over, and Old Town started to put its ciders in cans, a more accessible format for many than 750 ml bottles. David also realized that the jump from national brand–style ciders to a bone-dry, 100 percent Albemarle Pippin ferment would be too great for many in his market, and so Old Town Cidery developed a selection of slightly sweeter, flavored ciders as a gateway.

In 2021, Old Town Cidery opened a tasting room, which—as a result of the ongoing COVID-19 pandemic—forced them into the unusual situation of having a completely open-air tasting room. The tasting room was referred to as the Cider Yard and occupied a space that had been used by several generations of Glaizes for their business activities. The initial lease on that space was for only a single year, with the option to renew, so after two years of the Cider Yard, Old Town Cider was forced to close its direct-to-public business. They are currently looking for an alternative venue in which to reestablish the Cider Yard, but until then, their ciders are available at several local pubs and markets, as well as pop-up events organized by the cidery.

As for their ciders, Old Town Cidery currently has six products, all of which include the names of the apples used on the can. The most popular cider in the range is Valley Roots, which is a blend of IdaRed, Pink Lady, Golden Delicious and York apples and tends to be on the sweeter side but still with a dry finish. Old Town Cidery does also have a single varietal, Pippin, which uses 100 percent Albemarle Pippins and showcases the classic lingering dry finish associated with that apple.

PATOIS CIDERS

Charlottesville

Many cider makers have one or two sources for the apples that provide the juice that becomes their cider: either they have their own orchards or they purchase pre-pressed juice from a commercial orchard. Patrick Collins and Danielle LeCompte, however, have taken a different path to sourcing fruit: they forage abandoned orchards and seedling trees anywhere within a two-hour drive from their Charlottesville base.

Having worked in the restaurant and wine retail businesses, Patrick and Danielle developed an interest in the world of natural wine, a style of wine that minimizes human inputs such as fertilizers and commercial yeasts. It was when they stumbled upon an abandoned orchard in western Albemarle County that they decided to follow their interest in natural wine into the world of cider. In 2019, they started Patois Cider and released their first selection of natural ciders.

Having started with very limited funding, Patois is one of the few cideries in Virginia not to maintain a tasting room, preferring to sell direct to restaurants and retailers, as well as some online sales through their website. There was, however, also an ideological reason behind not wanting to start a "second business," which a tasting room inevitably becomes: Patrick and Danielle believe strongly that cider needs to become more of an everyday part of food culture in Virginia and that consumers benefit from it being available outside the curated environs of a tasting room. As Patrick himself puts it, "Cider needs to be more frequently encountered in a retail or restaurant setting, and cider needs to work harder on becoming a part of everyday food culture."[75]

Coming from a wine-centric background, Patrick and Danielle integrate many of the ways of winemaking into their cider making, such as fermenting and aging in wooden barrels, mostly neutral French oak but also black locust. They also practice the traditional riddling and disgorging of their bottled ciders, in the same manner as the winemakers of Champagne. As well as making cider in the *méthode ancestrale*, they also use continuous fermentation, a process of adding freshly pressed juice to an existing fermentation, and a variation on the solera system, where a portion of fermented cider is held back and blended with the following year's fermentation and so on each subsequent year.

At the heart of the Patois range of cider is a project called Bricolage, a cider made from approximately one hundred varieties of apple: some crab, some heirloom and some seedling apples. The harvest is taken from the more mountainous parts of Augusta, Albemarle, Nelson and Highland Counties. Each year's cider is an expression of the impacts of location and how the climate unfolded through the growing season as much as of the apples themselves.

Infinite Canon, an example of the Patois interpretation of the solera system, is made from a blend of Grimes Golden, Stayman, Arkansas Black and York apples from Rappahannock County, combined with the "perpetual reserve" that is the basis of a solera approach. Drinking the

The Bricolage Perpetual Reserve barrel at Patois Cider, where odds and ends meld together to make great cider.

resulting cider is almost like viewing a family tree, where you can see the traces of the past, with each year adding something new to the ongoing blend from the same trees.

Despite the fact that projects like Bricolage and Infinite Canon are core to the work Patrick and Danielle are doing at Patois, they do also produce a selection of "single site" ciders, usually also as single varietals. Of these ciders, none is more steeped in the history of Virginian cider making than Bent Mountain, so named for the plateau just south of Roanoke, on which a former commercial orchard of well-established Albemarle Pippins has been left to grow feral, at elevations around the three-thousand-foot mark.

While there is no tasting room to visit, local Charlottesville wine and craft beer stores keep Patois Cider in stock, and it is also possible to order bottles through their website for shipping to thirty-nine states, as well as Washington, D.C.

POTTER'S CRAFT CIDER

Charlottesville

Founded in 2011, Potter's Craft was a pioneer in the Virginia cider scene: one of the first to focus on traditionally made cider available on draft rather than purely in bottles. In what is perhaps a well-worn story, founders Dan Potter and Tim Edmond came to cider making from a base of having been home brewers while at college together. Indeed, Dan and Tim's initial plan was to start a farmhouse brewery, growing hops on-site and upscaling their home-brewing skills to a more professional level. However, disaster struck when the farm on which they had planted hops was flooded. With all their homebrew equipment intact, though, and with a source of freshly pressed apple juice, they decided to give making hard cider a go. The result was a cider unlike anything they had tried up to this point: dry, intensely fruity and with a sharp acid bite in the finish. Thus, beer was abandoned in favor of cider.

From that initial batch of homemade hard cider, they developed their flagship, and signature, cider, Farmhouse Dry, which is a blend of Albemarle Pippin, Virginia Winesap and GoldRush apples. Although initially known for a classic, traditional style of cider, Potter's Craft is more than willing to look beyond the apple for flavor components. When stepping beyond the well-worn pathways of traditional cider and trying something new, such as

Housed in a converted Episcopalian church, Potter's Craft Cider's tasting room is a timeless reminder of Virginia's original craft beverage.

adding grapefruit and hibiscus flowers to the cider, or when looking to the craft beer world by using modern hops such as Mosaic, Nelson Sauvin or Cashmere, Potter's Craft still lives by the mantra that you can't make good cider without good apples. As such, they use many of the staple varieties beloved of the Virginia cider industry, such as Albemarle Pippin, Virginia Hewes Crab and Harrison, having a range of single varietals that pays homage to those cultivars.

For Potter's Craft Cider, being a local company is about more than just location: it is an ethos that infuses everything they do as a company, and so they use exclusively apples grown in Virginia, as well as sourcing many of their ingredients from local farms and growers.

Today, the cidery has a tasting room located just off Route 29 as it heads south from Charlottesville, housed in a stone-built former Episcopalian church that is an absolute haven for fans of ecclesiastical architecture. The tasting room also has a spacious cider garden seating area with views down the Moore's Creek valley along wooded hills, where you can try a curated flight or order cider by the glass or bottle to enjoy on-site.

SAGE BIRD CIDERWORKS

Harrisonburg

It's a common story among many of the new generation of cider makers in Virginia: they start out in the home brew community and eventually decide they want to turn their passion for fermentation into a business. It is a story repeated with Zach and Amberlee Carlson of Sage Bird Ciderworks in Harrisonburg. Their first attempt at fermentation, which they admit was an attempt to save money as newlyweds with limited finances—as Zach points out, "It's cheaper to make your own alcohol than to buy it"—was making mead flavored with orange and cinnamon.[76] Zach happily owns up to the fact that despite following all the advice they sought, the outcome was terrible.

However, Zach and Amberlee had become devotees of fermentation, and having identified some of the areas where they went wrong with mead, they moved on to their next project: making cider. With some beer kits lying around, Zach took the equipment for brewing beer and used it to make cider, as they had access to juice. That initial single-gallon batch was "not great, but it was better than the mead." From that first gallon, Zach's cider making grew: from five gallons at a time to eventually having "many five-gallon carboys," in which he would make two hundred gallons of cider a year, the legal limit per household for home brew in the United States.[77]

Delving ever deeper into the world of fermentation, Zach and Amberlee eventually purchased an antique screw press, which they restored and then used to start pressing apples themselves rather than buying juice pre-pressed. At the time, they would purchase apples from Glaize Orchards in Winchester, just an hour up the road, as Glaize was growing the kind of apples Zach liked working with; it is a relationship that has continued into their professional cider making.

With the encouragement of friends, Zach and Amberlee started to enter cider competitions, picking up awards along the way and making it clear to them that their hobby had the potential to become their livelihood. In preparation for the possibility of starting a craft beverage business, Zach took courses at Oregon's Portland State University, after which he felt there was a real possibility that such a cider venture might work.[78]

Thus it was that in early September 2020, Zach and Amberlee opened their cider bar, in downtown Harrisonburg. Being the kind of people who like to do things themselves, they spent much of the year before opening renovating the cider bar and learning the practicalities of running a cidery. They also absorbed many of the lessons that other hospitality businesses had had to learn the hard way during the COVID-19 pandemic. As such, they paid special attention to their outdoor spaces, making sure that as people made their first tentative steps back toward something approaching normality, they would be comfortable, mentally as much as physically.

The initial taproom opened with five ciders on tap, four of which are still made today, including flagships Dry River Reserve and Sweet Shenandoah. Such was the response to their cider that just two weeks later, Sage Bird needed to purchase an additional fermenter to meet demand. Today, there are nine taps as well as bottled options available, such as their two pommeaux, ciders fortified with apple brandy in the vein of a port or sherry, which make for delightful after-dinner drinks. Sage Bird has also started a small orchard outside of Harrisonburg with the intention of using the fruit they grow for an estate vintage cider.

While Zach's approach to cider making leans more toward traditional ciders, he also enjoys the potential for creativity in adding ingredients like spices, hops and honey. However, his aim is to have a clean fermentation where the process takes a back seat to the flavors of the fruit itself; therefore, he predominantly uses champagne yeast, though Sage Bird's Spanish-style cider employs a wild fermentation in keeping with that tradition.

Sage Bird's ethos is very much that to make good cider, you need to have good cider apples, so they work with local orchards to source the apple varieties that are ideal for making the dry ciders they prefer. Naturally, that means using many of the standard varieties that Virginia cideries use: Virginia Hewes Crab, Black Twig and Albemarle Pippin. In particular, though, Zach has a fondness for the Virginia Hewes Crab—as he calls it, the "best cider apple coming out of Virginia," especially for its balance of acid and tannins.[79] Zach notes that a peculiar feature of the Virginia Hewes Crab apples he gets from Glaize Orchards is particularly appealing to him: the presence of water core. Water core is a buildup in the fruit of naturally occurring sorbitol, which is an unfermentable sugar and therefore remains in the cider after fermentation is complete, adding a fuller body and sweetness to an otherwise bone-dry cider.

At the end of the day, for Zach, the foundation of Sage Bird is the apple itself. As he comments, "If you can't taste the apple, why make cider?"[80]

SLY CLYDE CIDERWORKS

Phoebus, Hampton

In 2018, brothers Tim and Doug Smith came to the realization that the one-hundred-year-old brick-built house that had been the childhood home of their grandfather H. Clyde Smith needed to be either torn down or completely renovated. Here was a house, within walking distance of the pier in Phoebus and the Hampton River, that in the previous century had played host to several businesspeople rooted in the community, including florists, funeral directors and cabinetmakers. Not wanting to see their grandfather's house consigned to history, they decided to pour their life savings into renovating it and to start a business there that would benefit the community.[81]

The community's heart, Sly Clyde's taproom in Phoebus is a place for people of all backgrounds to come together around a pint of cider.

As is the case with many places in Virginia, in particular in the eastern reaches of the commonwealth, Phoebus has seen plenty of historically significant events. Indeed, it was at Strawberry Banks Bay in Phoebus that the adventurers aboard the *Susan Constant* (including the Smiths' own ancestors), *Discovery* and *Godspeed* made their initial landing on the soil that would become Virginia, before sailing on to establish Jamestown. Just a few hundred yards away from Sly Clyde is where the *White Lion* and then the *Treasurer*, English privateer ships, would land in 1619 and trade Africans captured from a Spanish slave ship for supplies to make their journey back to England.

In the early twentieth century, the terminus for the railway line to Chicago was in Phoebus, so gangsters needing to get out of the metropolis for a while would find themselves in Virginia. Bars, saloons and the rowdy behavior that often went hand in hand with that scene, in tandem with Phoebus having long been home to several major military bases, meant that the economically depressed Phoebus community developed a rough-and-ready reputation.

With the house in need of renovation and a vision of putting some kind of community-focused business on the property, Tim and Doug Smith decided to open a cidery. Doug admits that he and his brother were not ardent fans of cider—it is, after all, perceived as a "mountain drink." But at the same time, there were already more than enough breweries in the area, it didn't need another restaurant and nobody in southeastern Virginia was making cider at that point. Convinced that they needed to do something for the community, Doug and Tim built the cidery that is Sly Clyde—named in honor of their grandfather, with a nod to his renowned sly smile and wicked sense of humor—in the renovated house in the heart of Phoebus.[82]

At the heart of the vision for Sly Clyde was to bring a fractured community together, to bring people who, perhaps inhibited by fear, didn't normally sit across from each other into a space where they could be themselves and have interesting conversations with a diverse range of people, whether folks from local religious orders or people from historically marginalized groups. The Smiths' vision of Sly Clyde was very much in the mold of the traditional British pub, the social heart of a community where people find common ground over a glass or two of cider.

When it comes to the cider itself, Sly Clyde's goal is to make cider that drinkers want, rather than trying to garner the praise of other cider makers. The Smiths' cider is very much in the modern vein, using additional flavor components such as blackberry, mint and honey, and they are committed to supporting local growers and producers as much as possible. While the majority of the juice they use comes from orchards in the mountains of Virginia, there are a handful of apple trees on the property that supply some fruit. Also on the land—which once belonged to a florist, so the soil is wildly over-infused with nitrogen—there is a massive fig tree, which provides fruit each autumn for a seasonal fig cider.[83]

Despite not being shy about using non-apple ingredients, Sly Clyde eschews the use of concentrates and other shortcuts to the process to ensure as clean a fermentation as possible. They package in cans rather than bottles because theirs is very much an unassuming cider for working communities, as well as beachgoers—so much so that Doug says while drinking a Sly Clyde cider, you "should never feel like you should lift your pinky."[84]

SON OF A BEAR CIDERS

Rapidan, Orange County

The McMahon family who owns and operates Son of a Bear Ciders are deeply proud of their Irish ancestry: the name of their cidery is a literal translation of their family name. They are also proud of their family's military tradition, with all their ciders reflecting their history in the United States Air Force.

Located on some of the most bucolic agricultural land in Central Virginia, at present, Son of a Bear does not have a tasting room that is open to the public, but their ciders are available through several "partner locations," including wine stores, brewpubs and garden centers.

Son of a Bear currently produces eight ciders, as well as a pair of cyzers that combine their cider with mead. Their signature cider is Bear Force One (referencing the official aircraft of the president of the United States), a semidry blend of locally grown apples. For those with a sweeter palate, there is Rivet Bear Amber, which is aged in oak barrels to extract vanillin from the wood and give a semisweet roundness to the cider. For fans of ciders with additional fruit flavors, Son of a Bear's range includes infusions of strawberries, rhubarb and cranberry, among others.

TRODDENVALE AT OAKLEY FARM

Warm Springs, Bath County

Deep in the ridges and mountains of Bath County sits historic Oakley Farm, one of the first farms in the Warm Springs Valley, dating from the 1830s. From the very beginning, the farm has played host to orchards, with scattered remnants of those pioneer plantings still clinging on to the mountains and life, though they are coming to their end.

In 2018, the present owners and custodians of the farm, Will and Cornelia Hodges, bought Oakley from Will's grandparents and set about carrying on the work of preservation through farming and, with Troddenvale as the vehicle, making cider. They started in 2019 with the planting of two thousand trees over four acres of the property, recognizing an opportunity to elevate the status of cider in Virginia and the wider United States. Will also believes that the demise of cider in the postindustrial era has given this generation of cider makers an opportunity to express themselves unencumbered by the weight of a particular tradition.[85]

At first, Troddenvale (which roughly translates to "valley road") relied on foraged fruit from seedling trees throughout Bath County; such seedling trees have a tendency toward the higher acid, tannin and sugar combinations so important to making quality cider.[86] On Oakley itself, there are about forty

This way to the Troddenvale Cider Bar, where only good things await.

seedling trees, bearing fruit that doesn't necessarily have a name—or if it once did, that name has been forgotten. The Troddenvale ethos is that cider is a unique way to capture the personality of a place, that which in the wine world is referred to as terroir, though Will thinks of it as more than just the soil from which the fruit is grown: it is soil, climate, elevation, the very life of a place. Such cider bottles a snapshot of a place as it continues to evolve without human interaction.

When laying out their orchard, though, the Hodges made a conscious choice to not just grow apples that do well in the surrounding area but also focus on crabapples and varieties that thrive in locations with similar climates and elevations. The orchard is home to around twenty cider apple varieties drawn from the great cider-making regions of Europe—England, France and Asturias in Spain—including such exotically monikered varieties as Coloradona, Solarina and Reineta do Caravia, the latter of which is known for the high-acid juice that is essential to a Spanish-style cider.[87]

Before buying Oakley from his grandparents, Will worked in the California wine industry. He and Cornelia have brought a wine-informed ethos to the ciders they produce. In particular, they are committed to allowing the fruit to find its own highest expression through the cider. As such, they don't inoculate the pressed apple juice with commercial yeast, allowing the native wild yeasts of Warm Springs to do their thing in the wooden barrels they use for the fermentation itself.

Their aim is to minimize the cider maker's thumbprint, allowing the fruit, yeast and wood time to shine. This reductive approach means fermented cider often sits on the lees until Will feels the flavor has reached its peak; only then does he bottle. Troddenvale ciders will spend anywhere between four months and two years in the barrels. In general, Will and Cornelia prefer to ferment and age their ciders in French oak as it is less porous than other woods, which means less loss through evaporation, though it does impart a more pronounced spicy oak flavor than American oak.[88]

As well as the more traditional oak, Will and Cornelia also ferment in black locust wood. A tree native to Virginia, black locust has long been used in Europe as a more neutral alternative to the flavorful oaks; in the wine world, it is primarily used in white wine production. While black locust imparts less flavor, it does add some texture to the cider, as does the extended aging on the lees in terms of additional mouthfeel. The tight grain of black locust also maintains the freshness of the cider, and as it's a local species, readily abundant in Virginia, using it makes Troddenvale's footprint smaller.

Solera, the art of aging cider by continual blending to make the final product more than the sum of its parts.

Understated elegance is at the heart of Troddenvale, both in locale and in cider.

Over the course of a year, Troddenvale will release between fifteen and twenty ciders, with weekly tastings at the farm's Cider Bar. The Cider Bar or tasting room is one of the most charming spaces in which to drink cider; it feels akin to a British country pub, with all the hub of community sensibilities that implies. Open on Friday and Saturday afternoons, the Cider Bar has tastings available, as well as the option to buy cider by the glass or the bottle. With the exception of the first quarter of the year, Friday afternoons are what Troddenvale calls Foodlore Fridays, described as a "celebration of food, farmers, and community."[89]

While Troddenvale ciders are primarily vehicles of expression for the fruit that goes into them, there is a depth of thought and intentionality that Will and Cornelia bring to their understanding of, and philosophy regarding, cider. The Troddenvale House Cider is a case in point. Given their background in wine, Will feels that the adjective "house" has been debased, becoming essentially a proxy for the notion of "basic" rather than something excellent. It is their intention to turn that notion on its head by making House Cider the very best that Troddenvale puts out—and it is a simply magnificent cider.

TUMBLING CREEK CIDER

Meadowview, Washington County

Deep in the Appalachian southwest corner of Virginia, Tumbling Creek Cider is the coming together of four friends with a shared vision to create not just high-quality cider but also an economic ecosystem that could provide work and opportunities to their families and the wider community for years to come. It is a story that resonates deeply with the founding of Kelly Ridge Farms, where Tumbling Creek has its cidery and orchards.

The Kelly family has owned and farmed this land since their forefather Ezekiel migrated to Virginia from Ireland in the decades prior to the Revolutionary War. In 2012, having completed his education, Justen Kelly Dick, an environmental scientist by training, moved to the farm with his wife and family with the ambition to revitalize the land his family had stewarded for so many years. Already on the property was an acre of apple trees that had been planted by his grandfather. A year later, a neighboring farmer turned up with an apple press that had at one point belonged to Justen's grandfather, saying he felt it was only right that it come home. Today, the press is in the cidery's tasting room.[90]

Tumbling Creek Cider itself was established in 2018 when Justen united with three friends to start the business at the farm. The first of the friends to come on board was botanist Jerry Bresowar; together, he and Justen brought in Tom McMullen, who is today the primary orchardist, and Mark Finney. A year later, they set about creating the first of their orchards, having learned how to graft scions to the dwarfing rootstock they use to control the trees' size and the wait time to fruiting. Tumbling Creek's first year of pressing was in 2019, using apples purely from the sixty trees that make up the "old" orchard, planted by Justen's grandfather, which yielded five hundred gallons of juice.[91]

Today, as well as the old orchard, Tumbling Creek has planted an additional tall spindle orchard, giving them in total almost seventy apple varieties. Most of the trees are those grown specifically for cider production, including the Virginia faithfuls Hewes Crab and Harrison; they also grow Winesap, Limbertwig and Virginia Beauty. In the most recent pressing season, the cidery increased its yield tenfold, to five thousand gallons. As the main orchardist, Tom McMullen is committed to using as few artificial chemical inputs, such as insecticides, as possible.

Being located deep in Southwest Virginia and drawing on the rugged self-reliance of their forebears, the team Tumbling Creek is deeply committed to their locality and to being able to bring local products to market, as well as encouraging local production. Being an integral part of, and evangelist for, the local economy is very much a driving force behind the cidery, especially as it brings consumers and producers closer together.

As well as closing the circle between cider maker and cider drinker, Kelly Ridge Farms also takes advantage of this circular economy approach by feeding the pomace left over from pressing the apples into juice to the farm's Gloucester Old Spot pigs. Gloucester Old Spots themselves, being a breed with roots in the West Country of England, are no strangers to orchard life, and there is an old English tradition that they got their spots by being hit with apples falling from trees as they foraged for drops.[92]

In addition to producing traditional ciders, Tumbling Creek also makes a selection of flavored products using other locally sourced ingredients, including hops from Kelly Ridge Farm's own hop garden, blueberries from a neighboring farm and foraged spruce tips. Despite having only been producing since 2018, Tumbling Creek has already garnered several awards from prestigious competitions, including silver and gold medals from the Virginia Governor's Cup and the U.S. Open Cider Championship.

The cidery's flagship products are Moonshot and Ridge Runner. The former is a semidry cider that has a rich, full mouthfeel, pierced by the

Kegs of Tumbling Creek Cider at the cidery, ready to head to the tasting room in Abingdon.

high carbonation that makes it a deeply refreshing cider. In contrast, Ridge Runner is as dry as the desert, though still highly carbonated so that the dryness doesn't overwhelm the flavors of the traditional Appalachian cider apples and their bracingly tannic character.

In order to bring their heritage ciders to a broader audience, 2023 saw Tumbling Creek open the Taproom in nearby Abingdon, close to the town's farmers' market and visitor center. The Taproom operates as more than just a venue for trying Tumbling Creek's ciders and cider-based mixed drinks, as it hosts live music events, quiz nights and karaoke with an eye to being a place for people to gather over resolutely local cider.

WIDOW'S WATCH CIDER

Edinburg, Shenandoah County

Named for the architectural feature that sits atop the historic house where cider maker Mark Muse does his work, Widow's Watch Cider is the probably the smallest commercial cidery in Virginia and one of the very few that doesn't have a dedicated tasting room.[93]

Mark's pathway to establishing Widow's Watch Cider was essentially a winding, transatlantic quest to make a different alcoholic drink that eventually took a detour leading to cider. Having lived for many years in the Girona region of Catalonia, in Spain, Mark had developed a taste for the regional sparkling wine, cava. On moving back to the United States at the end of the twentieth century with his Catalan wife, Mark set about trying to re-create cava at their suburban home, initially by planting the appropriate grape varieties. At the same time, he and his wife planted several apple trees, which would eventually form the bedrock of the Widow's Watch orchard—sourced from, in a delightful circularity, Vintage Virginia Apples in Albemarle County, which would eventually morph into Albemarle CiderWorks.

Eventually, Mark and his wife decided that they wanted a larger property on which to grow their apples and grapes, so they purchased six acres and a house dating to just after the Civil War in Shenandoah County that is now home to their cidery. When they moved to the property, they transplanted about eight of their original trees, which flourished in their new home, unencumbered by other trees competing for sunlight. Finding it distinctly challenging to source the kind of grape juice necessary to faithfully re-create a Catalan cava, Mark started investigating the possibility of using apples,

Widow's Watch near Edinburg grows about 250 varieties of cider apple trees, all with long histories in North America.

realizing that Virginia is known as apple country and asking himself, "Why am I messing around with grapes?"[94]

With this realization, Mark again looked across the Atlantic, this time to the Normandy and Brittany regions of France, an area long known and celebrated for its cider heritage. In his research, he learned that in the nineteenth century, Normandy was famed for its apple-based sparkling wine, made in the *méthode champenoise*, which has all but disappeared in France today. It was this discovery of a dry, brut, apple-based champagne that proved to be the inspiration for Widow's Watch Cider and the realization of Mark's ambition to create a drink in the vein of cava. With a vision in mind, Mark extended the orchard to grow the trees that would give him the apples he needed.

When it came to choosing trees with which to form the orchard, Mark again turned to the Sheltons at Albemarle CiderWorks and their heirloom apple trees such as Virginia Hewes Crab, Albemarle Pippin and Roxbury Russet, all of which can trace their history to before the American Revolution. Such historical authenticity is a key feature of Widow's Watch Cider and an important touchstone for Mark himself in wanting to make the kinds of cider that have deep roots in Virginia.[95]

Widow's Watch only produces two ciders: the cava-inspired Brut Sparkling Virginia Apple Wine, made faithfully in the méthode champenoise, and Two George Cyder, a complex blend of seven prerevolutionary apple varieties that is influenced by the kind of ciders being made on the farms of Virginia in the colonial era. Unlike Brut, Two George is practically still, as ciders of that era would have been in the days before forced carbonation. However, the ciders share a common feature: the refreshing dryness and clean fermentation character that means both pair superbly well with full-flavored, rich food.

Being the smallest cidery in Virginia, with an orchard of about two hundred trees that supplies all its fruit, Widow's Watch doesn't maintain a dedicated tasting room. Instead, their ciders are available at select stores in the nearby town of Edinburg, such as the historic Edinburg Mill.

WILD HARE CIDER

Berryville, Clark County

Originally started by Jay and Coleen Clement, Wild Hare Cider initially opened its doors in 2015, in Bluemont. The Clements set out on a mission to change the way people thought about cider, using locally grown apples to craft traditional dry ciders that are a world away from the fare served up by major national cider brands. Eventually, they moved operations about fifteen miles up the road to Leesburg, where they still maintain a location.

With four locations across Northern Virginia, Wild Hare Cider is available in pub-style settings from Berryville to Fredericksburg.

In 2018, though, Jay and Coleen decided to sell the business to Jim Madaj, as they felt Wild Hare needed fresh investment to reach its fullest potential. In Jim's son, Justin, who'd studied cider production at Cornell's Craft Beverage Institute, there was a ready-made cider maker to step in and take the reins.

In the six years since Madaj purchased the company, Wild Hare has expanded to four locations across Northern Virginia: the Berryville tasting room, which is also where the cider is produced; the Fredericksburg Cider Pub; the Leesburg Cider Cabin; and finally, Warrenton Cider @ the Grainery.

Each of the locations harks back to a more rustic and easygoing time, when communities regularly gathered to drink and share the gossip of the day. As well as their regular lineup of ciders, cider maker Justin releases a small batch of special cider most weeks, and the locations are all used as community hubs, with events like bingo, live music and trivia night.

Like the vast majority of cider makers in Virginia, Wild Hare uses 100 percent Virginia-grown apples, mostly from the Shenandoah Valley. Their flagship is a "heritage dry" cider called Hatch that is fermented at cool temperatures and then aged for approximately twelve months prior to being released. For fans of the modern approach to cider, Wild Hare also produces several ciders that feature such ingredients as hops, orange peel and ginger.

WINCHESTER CIDERWORKS

Winchester

Sometimes an immigrant just wants a taste of home, to have that Anton Ego moment that takes them back to the simplicity and comfort of their childhood. When that home is in the East of England, the taste being hankered for will most likely be cider. That's why, in 2012, Englishman Stephen Schuurman started Winchester Ciderworks with the stated aim of making ciders that were drier than many of those he could find at the time—ciders like those from Suffolk, in the East of England.[96] In 2021, having garnered a decent-sized following, Stephen purchased the company outright from his founding partners and set about achieving his vision of spreading an understanding of English cider throughout Virginia and the Eastern Seaboard.

Before starting his cidery, Stephen had worked as a plastic engineer, and it was in that role that he first found himself in Virginia in the early 2000s, eventually deciding to stay. At the time, he was also an avid maker of wine and cider at home, having done so back in England as well. It seemed only natural, then, that as the Virginia wine industry was finding its feet and becoming more of a presence, he pondered the possibility of planting vines on the eight acres on which he lived. In preparation for that possibility, he attended viticulture courses in California, at UC Davis, as well as undertaking sensory training. However, with more and more wineries opening, he became reticent about becoming part of that scene.[97]

As chance would have it, next to his own land was an orchard, and so it occurred to him that given his dissatisfaction with the big-brand, excessively sweet ciders that were popular, he should make some scrumpy with some of the apples from the nearby orchard. It was on a trip home to Suffolk that Stephen managed to arrange some time to meet with the magnificently monikered Henry Chevallier Guild, owner of Aspall's Cyder, one of the UK's best-known traditional cideries. The advice he received was to focus on making a single cider, perfect it and then, five years later, make another cider and repeat. Heeding Chevallier's advice, Stephen spent a lot of time blending apple varieties and yeast strains to identify his one starting cider.[98] The outcome of that experimentation was Malice, the signature cider he continues to make to this day.

As Winchester Ciderworks makes Eastern English ciders, the freshly pressed apple juice is given plenty of time to ferment slowly, over a period of anywhere between four to five weeks. Once fermentation is complete, rather than rushing the cider to market, Stephens lets it age for a further six to nine months, which allows the acids to mellow and blend together, resulting in a cider that is crisp, refreshing, lightly sparkling and deeply quaffable, the kind of cider that comes in pints—proper imperial pints, of course.

While traditional Eastern English ciders are very much at the heart of Winchester Ciderworks, Stephen is not averse to adopting an American twist by adding fruit flavors, though their primary fruit flavor is distinctively English: the black currant. As it's an essential ingredient of the classic English "Cider

Winchester Ciderworks makes excellent ciders in the East of England style, and their new tasting room in the heart of Winchester is a must visit.

and Black," a blend of cider and black currant cordial, Stephen wanted to make a cider that incorporates the unique flavor profile of the black currant: reminiscent of raspberries and black cherries, with a slightly tart aroma, and lacking the heavy sugar load of a cordial. The result is 522, a reference to US Route 522, a major artery running through Frederick County.

As well as being passionate about cider, Stephen loves music, and he's melded these two passions into a collaborative cider with dark neo-folk band Bridge City Sinners.[99] The cider is infused with fresh elderberries, giving it a deep garnet color and a lingering fruity finish. Although Stephen does infuse fruit flavors into his ciders, he is adamant that those flavors come from actual fruit juice rather than extracts or other artificial adjuncts and flavorings.

Uniquely among Virginia cider makers, at least that I am aware of, Winchester Ciderworks produces ciders that are served through a beer engine, the traditional way of dispensing British real ale but also a common sight in England when it comes to cider.

In May 2024, Winchester Ciderworks opened up a new tasting room and restaurant in downtown Winchester, as the company had outgrown its previous location. Given that Winchester CiderWorks doesn't use clarifying agents such as isinglass, which is derived from fish bladders, their cider is naturally vegan friendly, so Stephen decided that they would also focus on good-quality vegan food to pair with it, as well as traditional dishes. With all their ciders being both vegan friendly and inherently gluten free, the goal is to have something for everyone to drink.

RECOMMENDED VIRGINIAN CIDERS

In an industry where producers are drawing inspiration from many diverse cider-making traditions—or, in some cases, from none at all, preferring to simply make something that expresses themselves through the apple—it is perhaps a Sisyphean task to even attempt to recommend particular ciders. Being something of a glutton for punishment, though, I offer up a few of the ciders that I particularly enjoy, several of which now make regular appearances in my fridge.

I am splitting up these recommendations into single varietal ciders, blended and flavored ciders, not because one or the other approach is inherently superior but rather for the sake of ease and organization. Likewise, no order of preference should be inferred from these lists.

Single Varietals

BIG FISH CIDER: VIRGINIA HEWES CRAB

Big Fish's Virginia Hewes Crab was the first single varietal cider that cider maker Kirk Billingsley ever produced, though it was not actually his intention to do so, having fermented the juice with wine yeast with a mind to incorporating it into Big Fish's blends. Kirk was so impressed by the resulting cider that he decided to bottle it. The cider itself pours a light golden color and has noticeable floral aromas as well as distinct notes of butterscotch. In terms of flavor, it is distinctly citrusy, with a stone fruit character that reminds me of peaches, and hints of cinnamon.

BUSKEY CIDER: VIRGINIA HEWES CRAB

It never ceases to amaze me that cider makers can take the exact same apple variety and produce completely unique ciders from it, a testament both to the work of the cider maker in coaxing the flavors they want out of the apple and to the influence of the growing conditions that particular year. Buskey's single varietal made with Virginia Hewes Crab is a rich yellow color and has aromas of flowers, bringing to mind the scent of mountain wildflower meadows in spring. Expect to find more fruit-forward flavors in Buskey's iteration: notably citrus peel, hints of strawberry and a touch of pear in the background. It's delightfully dry, zingy and refreshing.

ALBEMARLE CIDERWORKS: WICKSON CRAB

The Wickson crab apple is an absolute dream of a cider apple, and this is an absolutely stunning single varietal with an acid spiciness that makes me think of brut sparkling wines. On the nose, there is a definite sherbet character, coupled with a delicate bright lemon note. When it comes to flavors, the tropical fruit theme continues, with notes of pineapple, kiwi fruit and cantaloupe in the mix, elevated with a tart finish that brings all the flavors into sharp focus and makes this an excellent, refreshing cider.

TRODDENVALE: SPECIAL EDITION NO. 12

Tasting Special Edition No. 12, which is made with 100 percent Dolgo Crab apples and partly keeved, with Will at the Troddenvale tasting room in the mountains of Bath County was, quite literally, a revelation. The cider itself pours a delightful light red blush and has aromas of alpine strawberries, cranberry and maybe even a hint of lingonberry. The fruity aroma, though, gives no warning of what is to come: a full-on acid attack on the palate that is puckeringly dry and yet intensely flavorful as those berry notes fight through the acid. Pair this with similarly intense foods such as an extra-mature farmhouse cheddar or something rich like duck breast prosciutto.

CIDERS FROM MARS: SHADY LADY

Made with 100 percent Virginia-grown Harrison apples, Shady Lady showcases the workhorse of many a Virginia cidery, especially those producing more traditional ciders. In the glass, Shady Lady is a rich dark gold color, with stone fruit aromas (think peaches and nectarines) and a noticeable hint of apple blossom floating around in there as well. That fruity character carries over into the drinking, with more stone fruit notes, as well as some zingy berry notes that remind me of lingonberries, leading into the dry, citrusy zing in the finish that screams lemon zest.

CIDERS FROM MARS: KISMET

Kismet by name, kismet by nature. On a trip to Ciders from Mars in Staunton, my wife did a tasting to find out which cider she liked most, but there was just one on tap that day that was unknown to me: the Ruby Red Crabapple single varietal Kismet. It was delightful, and I have to admit I drank nothing else during that visit. It pours a beautiful, burnished gold, with slight aromas of rhubarb, which carry over into the taste department as well. The star of the show here, though, is the acidity: this is one sharp, tangy cider that scrapes your taste buds clean but at the same time leaves you just wanting more. It is simply fantastic.

HALCYON DAYS CIDER: OCCAM'S RAZOR

Occam's Razor states, quite simply, that the explanation that requires the fewest assumptions is usually the correct one, or the easiest answer is usually best. What could be an easier answer in the Virginia cider world than a single varietal of Virginia Hewes Crab? Halcyon Days' version of a Hewes Crab single varietal is a lovely golden color, with aromas of lemon zest, a hint of wildflower meadow and a bright acidity, which carries over into the flavor department, too. That citrusy note is mellowed slightly by some tropical fruit flavors, like pineapple, but fights its way forward again to leave the finish bracingly dry, lingering and demanding more.

Blended Ciders

SAGE BIRD CIDERWORKS: DRY RIVER RESERVE

Dry River Reserve is Sage Bird's flagship dry cider, available on tap at their Harrisonburg tasting room. It pours a pale yellow, with obvious carbonation, though without being wildly fizzy. On the nose, there are the classic Virginia citrus characteristics, like freshly zested lemon peel, and in terms of flavor, that fruity, citrus theme carries up, touched with a subtle floral hint and a depth that suggests petrichor—and like the air after rain, it is light and refreshing.

POTTER'S CRAFT CIDER: FARMHOUSE DRY

The original Potter's Craft Cider that they launched with back in 2011 is a blend of locally grown GoldRush, Old Virginia Winesap and Albemarle Pippin. It pours a sun-changing pale golden color, with plenty of life in the glass. Aromas of stone fruit (think summertime peaches and honeydew melon) dominate, while taste-wise it is nicely acidic, with hints of pineapple, clementine and subtle strawberry and a tart, cleansing effect on the palate. My personal heresy here is that Farmhouse Dry is a fantastic cider for drinking by the pint rather than from a dainty glass; if the pint is a twenty-ounce British-sized pint, even better.

TRODDENVALE: HOUSE CIDER

Will and Cornelia at Troddenvale are on a mission. Coming from a wine background, they've become frustrated with the way the term *house wine* has degenerated to such an extent that it means little more than a winery's cheapest, cheerfullest and least distinctive wine. They want their "House Cider" to be the exact opposite: the highest expression of both the fruit they use, from the Central Virginia and Southwest Virginia, regions, and themselves as cider makers. Made with an extensive list of the classic apple varieties that go into Virginia cider, including Harrison, Ashmead's Kernel, Arkansas Black and several others, this is a complex mélange of aromas and flavors, with notes of lemon blossom, thyme and honeydew melon. Given its entirely natural fermentation, this cider's finish is dry and noticeably tangy, with wisps of vanilla from the black locust barrels in which it is fermented.

BIG FISH CIDER: HIGHLAND SCRUMPY

This is a cider that, every year, I have to make a pilgrimage out to Monterey in Highland County for, braving the switchbacks of US 250 as it rises and falls through the George Washington & Jefferson National Forests. It was Highland Scrumpy that made me a fan of Big Fish Cider in general when I first tried it in the late summer of 2016. Made with nearly two dozen apple varieties—sourced from the local area around Monterey, many with no known names—Highland Scrumpy pours a crystal-clear gold, with aromas of pear and wildflower meadows. Taste-wise, you can tell right away that here is a cider made with a healthy dose of crab apple, with that classic acidic tang piercing through the mild sweetness that reminds me of cantaloupe. There is an earthiness to Highland Scrumpy, too, that makes it something I love to drink with a chunk of home-baked crusty bread and a wedge of good Gruyère cheese or even just sitting on the back deck enjoying it by itself.

SLY CLYDE CIDERWOKS: SUBMERSIVE

I'm going to let you in on a bit of a secret—well, OK then, not that secret if you know me. My taste in cider doesn't so much veer toward the dry side of the world as it positively jackknifes like an eighteen-wheeler on I-81. But I make an exception for Submersive from Sly Clyde. Sure, it's not as sweet as some ciders can be. It is, though, more than I usually go for, but here, it works. There is a freshness in the apple flavors that come through that I find delicious, with just a touch of tart sharpness that cleans the palate rather than coating it in slickness, as many a sweet cider will do.

LOST BOY CIDER: CELLAR SERIES SMALL APPLES

A tantalizing blend of acid apples—Ashmead's Kernel, Virginia Hewes Crab and Wickson Crab—this is as dry a cider as dry cider gets, and it simply sings. It pours a pale yellow with flashes of soft pastel green; given that the cider is unfiltered, it can also be cloudy if not poured gently from the bottle. That bright, acidic character presents in the nose as fresh cherries with a noticeable citric zing. When it comes to flavor, it is full of sharply acidic fruits—rhubarb, alpine strawberries and lime—yet the tannins add structure to the cider, giving it a fullness that almost, just almost, belies the dryness of the long, lingering finish.

ALBEMARLE CIDERWORKS: JUPITER'S LEGACY

Named in honor of Jupiter Evans, the enslaved man who was central to Thomas Jefferson's cider-making ventures at Monticello, Jupiter's Legacy is Albemarle CiderWorks' flagship and probably the most complex blend they produce, as it contains up to thirty different apple varieties, including Albemarle Pippin and Winesap. Added to the mix are a range of highly acidic crab apples. The cider itself pours a delicate golden color, with plenty of citrus on the nose, as well as a hint of floral character. For flavor, expect the classic Virginian crab apple zing of refreshing acidity, tempered somewhat by a rich tannic note that tastes somewhat like dulce de leche. Well-rounded and eminently sippable, this is a cider for the lingering hot days of late summer, just as the leaves are starting to turn.

CASTLE HILL CIDER: LEVITY

Levity is a unique cider, not just in Virginia but throughout the United States, as it is fermented in a Georgian-style terracotta vessel called a qvevri. The qvevri are buried underground, with just the opening aboveground, and the juice that goes into the vessels ferments naturally with its own yeast. Lightly sparkling and with a spicy nose, it has a delightful minerality in the mouth that plays nicely with the slight orange peel character.

DARING CIDER CO.: CRAB APPLE CIDER

This blend of a pair of crab apple varieties really is a meeting of the new and the old—Ruby Red and Virginia Hewes Crab, respectively—brought together to make a simply glorious whole. The classic citrusy aroma of the venerable Hewes is there in buckets, and the Ruby Red contributes additional berry-like aromas: think alpine strawberry, small yet punchy. In terms of flavor, yes, we have more citrus notes, lemons and a hint of lime in particular, as well as a complex, crisp apple character. Whether due to the presence of water core in the Virginia Hewes Crab, a common occurrence, or the mellow generosity of the Ruby Red, this cider has a touch more body than many a crab apple cider and yet finishes dry and crisply refreshing. The first time I had it, I fell into a reverie of wanting to pair it with my favorite farmhouse cheddar from England, as well as my homemade pear-based membrillo.

Flavored Ciders

WINCHESTER CIDERWORKS: SINNERS CIDER, WITH ELDERBERRIES

Made in collaboration with rowdy neo-folk band Bridge City Sinners, this elderberry-infused cider is a delightfully lurid bright red with distinct berry aromas mingling with a tart apple character that reminds me of the classic English dessert summer pudding. Taste-wise, the elderberries complement the tart, crunchy apple notes, with hints of sherbert, subtle ginger and a lingering dry finish that makes this cider a great alternative to a mimosa or sangria on a hot, sultry Virginia summer day.

BIG FISH CIDER: SHADY LANE SHANDY

There are shandies, a traditional English blend of beer with lemonade, and then there is Shady Lane Shandy, which squeezes into the cider some of the same flavors you would expect from an English shandy but with a base of superb Virginia cider. The cider is made with four apple varieties, Pink Lady, Stayman, Jonagold and Winesap, and once fermentation is complete, it's dry hopped with popular American hop varieties Citra, Centennial and Cascade, which give the cider a distinct grapefruit and hint of pine resin character. As if this was not enough, Kirk and the folks at Big Fish then convert the cider press into a lemon press and add freshly squeezed lemon juice to the mix, which elevates the hop flavor with an additional citric hit.

SAGE BIRD CIDERWORKS: STOCKING STUFFER, WITH JUNIPER AND TANGERINE

Stocking Stuffer, as the name suggests, is Sage Bird's winter seasonal cider, infused with juniper and tangerine peel, and it's quite frankly superb. It pours a beautiful clear yellow, laced with just the merest hint of green apple, but the aroma is a walloping great dose of Yuletide spice and a punchy orange note. When it comes to drinking, this is a definite sipper as the spice comes to the fore, with hints of clove, allspice and even some cinnamon, and the tangerine makes its presence felt as well, making you think of the clove-studded oranges so common in Yuletides past.

Chapter 3

THE FUTURE OF CIDER
IN VIRGINIA

WHAT DOES THE FUTURE HOLD?

In a little over four centuries, cider in Virginia has gone from being an essential staple of life for every class of inhabitant, celebrated on the tables of noted men as much as drunk by the enslaved for hydration. It was then eschewed in favor of lager beer made at industrial scale, with even the apples that make it so distinctive derided as unfit for pig fodder, with the editors of *Southern Planter* recommending orchards grow pretty apples for the marketplace. As we come to the end of the first quarter of the twenty-first century, it is important to take stock, think about how far Virginia cider has come and wonder a little about where it is going.

Given that more and more people are becoming aware of the wealth of cultural history that is bound up in heirloom fruits and vegetables and the urgent need to save that history from oblivion, it would be easy to look into the future with unbridled optimism. In the fifteen years since I moved to Virginia, we have seen the number of active cideries blossom from a mere handful to close to fifty, and that number doesn't include wineries and breweries for whom cider has become a sideline. Cider has perhaps never been more available through supermarkets, and while those retailers do lean very heavily toward the modern, often adjunct-laden and flavor-infused ciders, it is at least pretty common for there to be one side of an aisle dedicated to cider. In the independent bottle shops, you will readily find both traditional and modern ciders on the shelves. With more than thirty dedicated cider barns and tasting rooms dotted around the commonwealth, cider hasn't been so easily available since the drink's heyday in the middle of the nineteenth century.

In speaking with cider makers and orchardists throughout Virginia, I asked them to talk a little about where they see Virginia cider going in the next few years, and as would be expected, they gave me varying perspectives, though some common themes emerged.

At present, cider finds itself almost torn between two worlds, with both craft beer and wine making claims for cider to be an adjacent product. The divergence is pretty stark, with the modern, flavored ciders bearing a strong resemblance to craft beer and traditional ciders tending to be more akin to wine. As more and more breweries and wineries add a line of cider to their product ranges, this divergence will likely only become more distinct. There is, however, crossover that makes it impossible to really say that there are two cider worlds at the moment, especially given that many cider drinkers enjoy both types on their own merits under the broader aegis of "craft cider."

There is, however, a major difference between traditional and modern ciders when it comes to the apple varieties being used. Traditional cider makers have a clear preference for the older apple varieties that we have mentioned many times in this book, names like Virginia Hewes Crab, Harrison and, of course, the Albemarle Pippin. Meanwhile, ciders being produced in the modern vein use apple varieties such as Granny Smith, which has a flavor profile that many people are accustomed to.

As Diane Flynt at Foggy Ridge Ciders points out, "It is one thing to grow cider apples; it is something quite different to grow apples for cider."[100] Growing Virginia Hewes Crab is all good and well, but if the apples are harvested before they are fully ready to be pressed, the resulting cider is not a full expression of the apple.

With ever-increasing pressures on orchards to grow apple varieties for the supermarkets, storing them in low-oxygen environments to be packed on demand at any time of the year, it is hardly surprising that growing apples for cider is the pursuit of a dedicated few, even in one of the major apple-growing states.

Being a product of agriculture, cider is also at the mercy of our changing climate. For apple trees to produce fruit, they need a certain number of "chill hours" to have a complete dormancy cycle. Each variety is different, but the range is generally between six hundred to eight hundred hours. As winters in Virginia become milder, and wetter, it is becoming difficult for orchards to get the necessary number of hours of temperatures below forty-five degrees Fahrenheit. As a result, trees flower earlier than usual, and in the event of a cold snap, it is possible to lose vast swathes of the apple crop, as happened in the winter of 2023.

Up and down the Allegheny Highlands, a milder-than-usual winter saw trees bud and flower in early April, several weeks ahead of schedule. As many a Virginia gardener knows, it is folly not to expect some cold weather in the early spring, sometimes even in the middle of the season. With fruit set, a spring cold snap happened in May 2023, pouring cold Arctic air over the mountains, which sank into the valleys and utterly destroyed the crop. In some regions, such as Highland County, the estimated crop loss was between 90 and 95 percent. The trees that did manage to produce fruit were those at higher elevations; without them, several of the cider makers featured in this book would not have had apples to press in the fall of 2023.

There is a nugget of mountain wisdom that says if you get two crops in five years, you are doing well; climate change promises to put that wisdom to the test.[101] An interesting aspect of many of the trees that survived the biting cold of those few days in May is that they tended to be seedling varieties, those that were the product of random chance, adapted to the higher elevations in which they grow rather than manipulated for a consumer-centric perception of beauty.

Several cider makers I spoke to also suggested that, given that cider today doesn't have the mass appeal of beer, the industry as it stands in Virginia is already in a state of saturation and consolidation is a very real possibility. A common theme that emerged from these conversations was that there are essentially only two paths available to the cider maker now: "macro or micro," as one cider maker phrased it. There would seem to be very limited scope for a middle ground between mass production, with the distribution footprint it entails, and the niche artisanal cider maker selling predominantly to their local market. While couched in very modern terms, in some ways, this is a return to the pre-industrialization paradigm, where local ciders were made for local consumption and cities tended to import cider from rural regions or even from northern states. The key difference here, though, is the ease of transport and the importance of agritourism to Virginia, where it generated $2.2 billion in "total economic activity" in 2015.[102]

In speaking with Diane Flynt, it became clear to me that perhaps the key players in the future of cider in Virginia are not necessarily the cider makers themselves but rather the orchardists. It seems obvious to say that the orchard is the birthplace of cider; as Diane writes in *Wild, Tamed, Lost, Revived*: "Before cider, there were apples."[103]

Ever since the founding of Foggy Ridge Cider, it has been part of their mission not just to make great traditional cider but also to advocate for commercial orchards to grow heirloom cider apples, despite the challenges that poses. Cider apples, being mainly either bittersweets or bittersharps, have little market value outside of cider making. There are very few people who are happy to have a bite of a highly acidic apple such as the Virginia Hewes Crab or take on the tannic bitterness of a Dabinett, for example.

As has, hopefully, become evident, not all apples are created equal when it comes to making traditional cider that is an expression of the fruit. The complex balancing act of sugar, acid and tannin means that there are some apple varieties that simply don't have what it takes to make cider. And so, with that fact in consideration, the role of the commercial orchard in the viability and continued development of the cider industry in Virginia is central.

It is a fact that the vast majority of cider makers in the commonwealth do not have their own orchards, especially in urban centers such as Richmond and Northern Virginia. Even the cider makers with their own orchards are not generally in a position to rely purely on their own fruit.

When first developing the Foggy Ridge orchard and cidery, Diane made a very conscious decision that she would only grow apple varieties she could not purchase elsewhere, which in the 1990s and early 2000s meant growing the varieties whose names have popped up time and time again: the long-lost Harrison, Virginia Hewes Crab and Dabinett from England.[104] It is a philosophy that Diane's longtime cider maker Joceyln Kuzelka has incorporated into her own work at Daring Wine and Cider Co.: to support local agriculture by growing only what she cannot buy nearby.[105]

A phrase that Diane used several times as we talked was: "It is one thing to grow cider apples; it is something completely different to grow apples for cider." Throughout the history of cidermaking, the requirement for apples to "mellow" has been a constant theme. A mellow apple is one that is completely ripe; it is one where the balance of sugar, acid and tannin has reached its zenith; it is one that is ready for the press. This necessity is why the orchardist, whether at one of the cideries with its own trees or at a commercial operation, is so important to the present and future of cider in Virginia. Pick a cider apple too early or too late and the characteristics that make it a cider apple, as opposed to a dessert apple or a cooking apple, are degraded, and the resulting cider will not meet the vision of the cider maker.

The primacy of the orchard and those tending to the trees that produce the apples is also something Will Hodges at Troddenvale is very much aware of:

I believe the future of Virginia cider will be molded by the efforts to grow cider fruit. The capacity and dimension of this industry's production is inherently tied to its ability to grow the fruit it requires. Although it will always be easier and sometimes outright necessary to simply outsource that dimension of a cidery, I really believe the industry's growth and future lies within those willing to make the effort to grow the right fruit and focus on how best to do so.[106]

To David Glaize of Old Hill Cidery, himself a fourth-generation apple farmer in the Winchester region, the future of apple growing seems bright right now as he fields more and more calls for pre-pressed juice from cideries around Virginia, as well as faraway states such as Minneapolis, Maine and Texas. In particular, he noted that "cider makers in New England love southern apples, in particular the classics, Virginia Hewes Crab, Harrison and Arkansas Black."[107]

David also mentioned the importance of apple growers thinking strategically about the crops they grow and how they choose to process them with an eye to making sure that they can keep the trees on the land by adding value to the raw apple crop. He believes that the ability to adapt, both to climate change and the continually shifting whims of consumer taste, will stand orchardists in good stead for whatever the coming years have in store.

With slim margins in the apple-growing world and an ever shrinking number of orchards in Virginia—only a century ago, there were fifteen growers just in the Winchester area; today there are five—it is vital to protect what remains and set it up for the future.[108]

Perhaps the pressing need for cider in Virginia, as identified by several of the cider makers I spoke to for this book, is to reconnect people to the history of cider in the state. Several generations of Virginians now have grown up understanding the term *cider* to mean a freshly pressed but then pasteurized product that comes in gallon jugs in the fall, has no alcohol and uses sweet apples.

As we have seen, this is actually a departure from the real history of cider, both in Virginia and the broader United States. In this context, the tasting rooms of cideries are a vital avenue for educating people about the true nature of cider and its depth of history in the commonwealth of Virginia and for reconnecting them to America's original craft beverage. It is, therefore, very telling that the vast majority of Virginian cideries, regardless of which of the three camps I identified earlier they fall into, tend to have at least one or two dry ciders, either as single varietals or a blend of heirloom cider apple varieties.

One of the most interesting perspectives to have cropped up several times concerns the relationships between cider and beer and wine. The law in Virginia is quite clear on this point:

> *"Cider" means any beverage, carbonated or otherwise, obtained by the fermentation of the natural sugar content of apples or pears (i) containing not more than 10 percent of alcohol by volume without chaptalization or (ii) containing not more than seven percent of alcohol by volume regardless of chaptalization. Cider shall be treated as wine for all purposes of this subtitle, except as otherwise provided in this subtitle or Board regulations.[109]*

Cider in Virginia is, therefore, legally wine. Culturally, though, it is often a bridge from beer to wine and back again, as Henway Hard Cider's Scott Spelbring points out: "Cider has the lifestyle of beer with the finesse of wine."[110]

This ambiguity allows the cider makers of Virginia immense latitude in designing and delivering their products to the consumer, much to the consumer's benefit, as there is quite literally a cider for every taste, made invariably from apples grown in Virginia. What is not legally ambiguous is that cider, minus an adjectival epithet, is alcoholic, again pointing to "sweet" cider as the historical aberration.

Finally, one thing that has become evidently clear to me both as a cider drinker and in meeting orchardists and cider makers across Virginia is just how much room for improvement in the general public's understanding of cider still exists—especially regarding cider's place as an artisanal agricultural product with distinctly premodern flavor profiles that many first timers, perhaps, find challenging. To quote Scott Spelbring: "It is often the flavored cider that gets people through the door, and from there, we can talk about the roots of cider in Virginia and put the history in front of them, in a glass."[111]

VIRGINIA CIDER: THE MAKERS' VIEW

We live in the locavore age, especially when it comes to the craft beverages we choose to drink, which raises the question: What exactly is "Virginia cider"? What differentiates cider made in Virginia from that which is made in England, Spain or even New York? Why should we care that Virginia cider is a thing, assuming that it even is a thing, much less a thing worth seeking out, enjoying and perhaps protecting?

At its most basic level, it is possible to argue that Virginia cider is, simply, just that: ciders made in the commonwealth of Virginia. However, after over four hundred years of apples being pressed into juice and then fermented, whether legally or otherwise, in the state, is there in Virginia cider a tradition to be cherished just as much as in Somerset or Asturias? Perhaps, though, the situation is that there *was* a definable tradition, but nearly a century of industrialization, prohibition and the rise of lager beer as an urban alternative to cider has created a rupture between cider and the people?

In surveying the current state of the cider-making industry in Virginia, I've identified three major camps, or groupings, of cider makers: the traditionalists, the modernists and the in-betweeners. That is not to say that any one approach has more value than any of the others or that one particular strand in the weave that is cider in Virginia is more authentically "Virginian." While I feel that the three camps image has some value, as with any analogy, it inevitably falls down at some point, especially as while cider makers may predominantly exist within a given camp, they are more than happy to cross over and try something from one of the other camps from time to time. Every cider maker I spoke to in researching this book has mentioned how much they value the ability to experiment and get creative, as well as the great sense of comradery that exists within the cider scene here. As David Glaize said to me, "Everyone does it differently, and that is cool and exciting."[112]

Regardless of which camp a cider maker may appear to fall into, there is a shared sense among them that Virginia is special when it comes to apple growing and that this is reflected in the ciders produced here. According to the Virginia Apple Board, about 6 billion bushels of apples are grown in Virginia each year, a bushel being approximately 45 pounds, which equals 270 billion pounds of apples. The majority of those apples are grown in mountainous regions, which have long growing seasons where the days are warm and the nights are cool, perfect conditions for bringing apples to a full ripeness, which develops complex flavors that are ideal for cider. To quote Scott Spelbring: "We grow some damn fine apples here in Virginia and continue to pave the way in concentrate-free, true ciders with apples from our backyard."[113]

Without fail, every cider maker I have met and spoken with commented on how their ciders are made with 100 percent Virginia-grown apples, showing the importance of highlighting the fruit that is grown here.

As we have seen and come back to several times, there are, though, some apple varieties that have a special resonance with cider makers here in Virginia, in particular those apples grown specifically for cider—Virginia Hewes Crab, Harrison and Roxbury Russet, to name a few—apples that have long histories of their own of being grown and used in cider making in Virginia. As with the Spanish traditions from Asturias and the Basque Country, maybe a defining feature of Virginia cider is the use of such historic cider apples. Chuck Shelton at Albemarle CiderWorks would certainly say so: "I would say that the quintessential Virginia cider apple would be Hewes Crab. It has been around for centuries and is at the forefront of the revival of cider. However, Harrison deserves recognition as well."[114]

A sense of nostalgia is likewise a common thread running through the Virginia cider world. Many consumers have a deep personal sense of belonging when it comes to apples and orchards, with many households having had an apple tree in the backyard or trips to pick-your-own orchards as a common feature of childhood. When I spoke with Allen Crump of Richmond's Buskey Cider about cider and its relation to the craft beer world, he commented, "Cider was there to blend the nostalgia and heritage of apples with the innovation of craft beverages. We have a deep, rich heritage of apples and cider, great apples to work with and a customer base who actively seek out well-made and interesting products."[115]

For some, that nostalgia is absolutely essential in defining what constitutes a Virginia cider, specifically looking back to the table drinks of the seventeenth and eighteenth centuries, when cider making in Virginia was arguably at its zenith. Mark Muse of Widows Watch, probably the smallest cider maker operating in Virginia today, puts it thus:

> *I place the emphasis on the heritage of the apple and insist on apples that reflect the centuries of cider making in the commonwealth. A "real" authentic Virginia cider is made of those apples that made up Jefferson's and Washington's daily drink: Hewes Virginia Crab, Old Virginia Winesap, Albemarle Pippin and a host of others.*[116]

It is clear, then, that although the cider makers in Virginia are all expressing their creative personas in the ciders they produce, whether they be a single varietal ferment of Virginia Hewes Crab or a wild fermentation drawing inspiration from the Spanish sidra tradition, each cider maker featured in this book is drawing from the same wellspring of four hundred years of apple growing and cider making in Virginia.

As such, there is clearly some element of a regional identity that can be found in the ciders of Virginia, a product of the unique climate and growing conditions that exist here. Patrick Collins of Patois Cider, who uses exclusively foraged fruit from abandoned orchards and seedling trees, notes: "We are a warm-climate growing region, which lends a richness and body to a dry cider that I don't often perceive in New England or European ciders."[117]

Such warmer conditions are conducive to the development of water core—an overproduction of the unfermentable sugar sorbitol—as a heat stress response in many of the varieties grown in Virginia, in particular our old friend Virginia Hewes Crab, a characteristic that is valued by several cider makers featured here. However, it is clear that even within Virginia, the growing conditions of a given orchard make a vital difference in the final product. A single varietal of Virginia Hewes Crab from the mountains of Southwest Virginia will be markedly different from the same varietal grown in the flatter, hotter regions to the east of the Blue Ridge Mountains.

Regionality, growing conditions and climate, then, are clearly pivotal to any attempt to define "Virginia cider," and that forces us to recognize and consider the possible impacts of climate change on the apples that go into making cider, as we have touched on elsewhere. As the climate continues to change, the apples that can be successfully grown in Virginia will likewise change and adapt; from that perspective, the future is deeply uncertain.

While considering the notion of regionality and the impact of climate change on apple growing—and by extension, cider making—it is also worth considering the concept of terroir. So far throughout this book we have only considered two of the main influences on terroir: climate and the tradition that a cider maker draws inspiration from. There are, however, two additional influences, and here we have to think about geology as we consider the role of soil and terrain. To entirely oversimplify it, not all soils have evolved equally when it comes to growing conditions for apples, and different elevations will develop different flavors in the very same apple variety.

In her book, Diane Flynt notes that orchardists in Nelson County growing the same apples she was growing in Carroll County, a couple hours' drive away, developed wildly different flavors and even chemistry. However, she admits, "When I had the chance to taste a nearby neighbor's Grimes Golden side-by-side with the same variety from my orchard, I was shocked. Same apple. Same harvesttime. Same elevation. Entirely different flavor."[118]

Clearly, then, the location of an orchard has an impact on the flavors that the cider maker will be able to coax out of the fruit they are using. Many of the orchards currently growing cider apples in Virginia do so on top of limestone bedrock, whether they be in Winchester, Bath County or Southwest Virginia. However, it is not the case that apple growing in Virginia has been limited to mountain country. Remember that within twenty years of establishing Jamestown, it was a legal requirement for colonists to plant orchards, and European settlement of the Shenandoah Valley was still a century away. The early orchards of Virginia, as mandated by the royal governor at the time, William Berkeley, would have been planted in soils with sand or gravel bedrocks, and still they thrived. It was also in these sand and gravel soils that the Virginia Hewes Crab had its origins, which demonstrates the supreme adaptability of apples to the various geologies they encounter, whether that means bedrock of limestone, sandstone or gneiss.[119]

Terroir as popularly perceived is likely too simplistic an understanding of the "complex interplay of climate, soil, geology, and viticulture, all of which influence the character and quality" of a cider, according to Lawrence Meinert, though the article referenced specifically concerns itself with wine. Yes, we can identify geologic similarities and differences between growing regions, but Meinert also points out that when it comes to the minerals in a soil, "most of the measurable trace elements have no sensory effect, and it is plant physiology, not geochemical composition of soils, that controls the ripening and sensory characteristics."[120]

So while we must remember that cider is unabashedly an agricultural product, it is too much of a stretch to call it entirely "natural." No apple has ever, at least as far as we are aware, leapt from the tree and pressed itself to squeeze out the juice that becomes cider. The human element in cider making is, therefore, central to any definition of cider in general and in our context Virginia in particular.

Within the cider industry of Virginia, almost entirely regardless of the tradition and cultural influences of the cider makers themselves, there is a strong undercurrent of nostalgia. Of the dozens of cider makers I met with and spoke to in researching this book, not a single one uses anything other than Virginian apples. To differing degrees of proximity from their cidery, that sense of taking pride in the apples of Virginia is common, whether they're using their own orchards, staying within the confines their county or sourcing apples from locations around the state.

On the importance of apples and a sense of nostalgia within Virginia cider, Will Hodges of Troddenvale comments:

I think Virginia cider is an evolving concept that is rooted in a deep history but is deservingly reinventing itself in a new century. Virginia cider to some degree should be defined by the apple varieties that have historically and effectively grown here—but in the same breath, it doesn't have to be.[121]

Virginia cider is that which is made by the cider makers of Virginia, and they are a diverse, eclectic group of people, each with a unique, powerful story about how they came to love cider and make it their life's work. Every business owner and cider maker I spent time with and spoke to on this journey is engaged, informed and deeply passionate about making the best ciders possible, in a way that is an expression of themselves and of the immense apple bounty that is part of Virginia's history, present and future.

I leave the final word on trying to define Virginia Cider to Doug Smith, owner of Sly Clyde Ciderworks: "What's more wonderfully Virginian than that? Travelers making our way through time, learning to craft the best beverages for our neighbors in the hopes that we might steal a bit of community around a common libation."[122]

GLOSSARY

The following list of common cider terms is intended as a reference for some of the terminology used in this book, as well as in the broader cider world.

ACID: There are two types of acid present in apples, malic and ascorbic. The main type is malic acid, derived from the Latin name for the genus of trees that includes apples, *Malus*. It is malic acid that cider makers are mainly interested in when it comes to making their products. Ascorbic acid, also known as vitamin C, is present in smaller amounts than malic acid when the apples are ripe and may also be the reason that Basque sailors who were drinking half a gallon of cider a day on their journeys rarely got scurvy.

APPLE: Apples are the star of the show: without them, there would be no cider. They are the fruit of the *Malus* genus of trees and shrubs, including domesticated, crab and wild apples. Apples are categorized as either culinary, dessert or cider, depending on whether they are intended primarily for cooking with, eating or turning into cider, respectively. Cider apples are further categorized by the Long Ashton Research Station based on their specific balances of acids and tannins as being:

- Bittersharp: high in tannin and acid, mostly used as cider apples
- Sharp: high in tannin, low in acid, mostly used as culinary apples
- Sweet: low in tannin, low in acid, mostly used as dessert apples
- Bittersweet: low in tannin, high in acid, mostly used as cider apples

GLOSSARY

BLEND: A type of cider that uses multiple apple varieties to achieve the flavor profile that the cider maker is looking for.

CHAPTALIZATION: Simply put, the process of adding fermentable sugars to the apple must in order to boost the eventual alcohol content of the cider. This process is more common among modern cider makers, with traditionalists using just the sugars naturally occurring in the apples they are turning into cider. The term is named for French scientist Jean-Antoine Chaptal, who described the process at the beginning of the nineteenth century.

CHEESE: Formed blocks of pomace from which apple juice is pressed.

CIDER: For the purposes of this book, cider is the fermented juice of apples. There is no internationally recognized single definition of cider, but in the vast majority of cider-producing countries, cider is an alcoholic beverage. Different traditions allow for varying amounts of apple juice to be used in "cider," ranging from 30 percent to the requirement that cider be entirely made from pressed apple juice.

DRY CIDER: The lack, or complete absence, of residual sugar in dry cider leads to the perception that the drink is not sweet. The majority of traditional ciders would be considered dry, as most of the sugar pressed from the apple is fermentable.

FERMENTATION: The process of yeast converting the sugar in the must into alcohol and carbon dioxide.

KEEVE: Keeving is a traditional process, often used in French cider making, whereby yeast is deprived of essential nutrients, in particular nitrogen, resulting in a slow, incomplete fermentation that leaves more residual sugars in the final cider. The process uses the natural pectin in the fruit combined with calcium to form a jellylike substance, known as *chapeau brun* due to its brown color, that floats to the top of the fermenting vessel. The end result is a sweeter and naturally clear cider.

MILL: The device that either crushes or chops the apples so that they are an appropriate size for pressing. *Mill* is an archaic term for the entire location where cider making takes place.

Orchard: A deliberately planted grove of apple trees. There are three main types of orchard in use today:

- Traditional: These tend to be older orchards, as this type has a lower fruit yield than modern orchards. Trees tend to be of standard size, upward of twenty feet, and can take a decade or more to fully start bearing fruit. Usually there are about sixty trees per acre in this system.
- Semi-intensive: Trees are grown on semi-dwarfing rootstocks, limiting their height to a maximum of fifteen feet. Usually there are about seven hundred trees per acre. Many Virginia cider makers' orchards are semi-intensive.
- Modern/intensive: Trees are grown on dwarfing rootstocks, which limits the height of the trees to about ten feet, often requiring trellising and irrigation. The benefits are greater yield per acre and only three or so years to a full crop. In an intensive orchard, there can be up to one thousand trees per acre.

Pearmain: A type of apple once spelled "permain" and known for its superior storing characteristics, mainly by virtue of being a rather hard apple. There are various theories as to the etymology of the term *pearmain*: nineteenth-century pomologist Robert Hogg believed the word was derived from the Latin phrase *pyrus magnus* in the medieval era and referred to apples that bore a resemblance to pears. He also suggested that the original pearmain was the "Winter Pearmain," which was first recorded in England around the year 1200, making it the oldest named apple variety in England. As romantic a notion as that is, the most likely etymology is that it comes from the Middle English *parmain*, which drew on the Middle French *parmaindre*, meaning "to last or endure."

Pippin: An apple that grew from a single seed, also called a seedling. The term *pippin* comes from the French word *pepin*, meaning "pip."

Pomace: Also called pulp. The fruit after it has been crushed or chopped in the mill. Occasionally this also refers to the mass of apple fresh that is left over after pressing. Pomace is traditionally used as a source of mulch along fence lines and a source for seedling trees, either as rootstocks or new varieties of apple.

POMMEAU: A specialty of Normandy that is becoming more popular with Virginia cider makers. To make pommeau, apple brandy is added to cider in order to increase the alcohol content to somewhere between 15 and 20 percent. Pommeau is, therefore, similar to fortified dessert wines such as port or sherry.

PRESS: The machine that applies pressure to the pomace in order to extract the juice. Traditional manual presses apply the pressure from the top and use a screw to increase it, thus extracting more juice. Many modern cideries, including several in this book, use hydraulic presses that use water to expand a membrane inside the core of the press to squeeze out the juice.

RUSSET: *Russeting* describes brown patches of rough skin on the surface of an apple. In some cases, this is an indicator of environmental stresses, such as extreme heat or a lack of water; in others, it is a natural feature of the cultivar. Russeting is often an indicator of an older variety of apple, as it has largely been bred out of modern cultivators designed to appeal to the eye. Apples that display this characteristic as a matter of course are referred to as russet apples and possess a sweet nuttiness. Examples of russet apples commonly in use for making Virginia cider are the Roxbury Russet and Ashmead's Kernel.

SCRATTER: A type of mill that uses toothed rollers to crush the apples.

SINGLE VARIETAL: A cider that is made from a single variety of apple. Many cider makers in Virginia produce single varietals using classic American cider apples such as Virginia Hewes Crab and Harrison.

SWEET CIDER: In the context of cider as a fermented alcoholic beverage, a sweet cider is one that has a higher level of residual sugar, whether through stopping fermentation before the cider reaches the "dry" stage or by back sweetening with fresh juice or another sweetener.

TANNIN: Tannins are substances in apples that produce an astringency in the final cider. Tannins also contribute to the mouthfeel, as well as increasing the perception of aroma in the cider.

WATER CORE: Commonly considered a flaw in dessert apples, water core can be of benefit to cider makers as it creates natural sorbitol in the apple.

Sorbitol is an unfermentable sugar and so leaves a trace of residual sugar in ciders made with water-cored apples, which adds to the mouthfeel of the cider.

YEAST: The hero of the story, yeasts are single-celled organisms that convert sugars in the must to produce alcohol and carbon dioxide. Yeast is found naturally on the skins of apples, and as such, there is no essential need to add yeast to the must. However, not all yeasts are created equal when it comes to producing flavorful ciders, and so some cider makers use commercially available yeast strains that have been selected for specific characteristics, including yeasts used in the wine and beer industries.

RECOMMENDED READING

The following books were either helpful in researching the history of apples and cider in Virginia or gave insight into the various international traditions that Virginian cider makers draw their inspiration from.

Brown, Pete, and Bill Bradshaw. *World's Best Ciders: Taste, Tradition, and Terroir.* New York: Sterling Epicure, 2013.

Flynt, Diane. *Wild, Tamed, Lost, Revived: The Surprising Story of Apples in the South.* Chapel Hill: University of North Carolina Press, 2023.

Forbes, Susanna. *The Cider Insider.* London, UK: Quadrille, 2018.

Hatch, Peter J. *The Fruits and Fruit Trees of Monticello.* Charlottesville: University of Virginia Press, 1998.

Jolicoeur, Claude. *Cider Planet.* White River Junction, VT: Chelsea Green Publishing, 2022.

Pucci, Dan, and Craig Cavallo. *American Cider.* New York: Ballantine Books, 2021.

Watson, Ben. *Cider, Hard and Sweet: History, Traditions, and Making Your Own.* Woodstock, VT: Countryman Press, 2013.

OUT AND ABOUT

This book is not really a travel guide; the main intention here is to tell the stories of the many diverse cider makers in Virginia today. Having said that, though, managing to get to more than thirty cideries up and down Virginia takes some logistical planning. In practical terms, it meant several overnight trips on weekends as well as several day trips to get to as many as possible in order to meet the cider makers and take pictures. In the spirit of having pored over maps trying to work out viable groups of cideries to visit in a given day, I would like to suggest the following groupings as being geographically feasible in a single day.

When initially trying to break things down, we identified five main "regions" that we would be visiting:

- Central Virginia
- Mountains
- Shenandoah Valley
- Coastal Virginia
- Northern Virginia

Where necessary, we broke regions down further and labeled them by the roads we would be traveling on or the locality we would be visiting, so I share with you these groupings in the order in which we visited them. However, I have included only cideries with tasting rooms. I am not going to give you directions; Google Maps is better at that than I could ever be.

CENTRAL VIRGINIA

Route 29

- Bryant's Cider and Brewery, Nelson County
- Blue Toad Hard Cider
- Bold Rock Cider
- Albemarle CiderWorks
- Potter's Craft Cider

Goochland/Louisa/RVA

- Coyote Hole Craft Beverages
- Courthouse Creek Cider
- Blue Bee Cider
- Bryant's Cider Tasting Room
- Buskey Cider

I-81 "South"

- Apocalypse Cidery & Winery
- Halcyon Days Cider Co.
- Ciders from Mars
- Sage Bird Cider

THE MOUNTAINS

- Tumbling Creek Cider
- Troddenvale at Oakley Farm
- Big Fish Cider

THE VALLEY

- Old Hill Cider
- Winchester Ciderworks

NORTHERN VIRGINIA

NoVA

- Cobbler Mountain Cellars
- Cider Lab
- Lost Boy Cider

Loudoun County

- Corcoran Vineyards & Cidery
- Henway Hard Cider
- Mt. Defiance Cider Barn
- Wild Hare Cider

Coastal

- Ditchley Cider Works
- Sly Clyde Ciderworks
- Back's Bay Farmhouse Brewing

NOTES

Chapter 1

1. William Harding Carter, *Giles Carter of Virginia: Genealogical Memoir by William Giles Harding Carter* (Baltimore, MD: Lord Baltimore Press, 1909), 90.
2. "Five Ways to Compute the Relative Value of a UK Pound Amount, 1270 to Present," Measuring Worth.com, https://www.measuringworth.com/calculators/ukcompare.
3. "Letter of Arthur Allen 1704 July 04," Library of Virginia, https://rosetta.virginiamemory.com/delivery/DeliveryManagerServlet?dps_pid=IE3446064.
4. Nicholas Spencer, 1682, as quoted in "Hard Cider's Mysterious Demise," accessed at https://mason.gmu.edu/~drwillia/cider.html.
5. Eliza Smith, *The Compleat Housewife* (London: J and J Pemberton, 1727).
6. Ibid.
7. Ibid., emphasis in original.
8. Edward Munford, "Overseer Agreement between Edward Munford and Turner Jackson, 1760 February 9," Special Collections, John D. Rockefeller Jr. Library, Colonial Williamsburg Foundation, https://cwfjdrlsc.omeka.net/items/show/1412.
9. *Virginia Gazette*, August 22, 1771, Special Collections, John D. Rockefeller Jr. Library, Colonial Williamsburg Foundation, https://cwfjdrlsc.omeka.net/items/show/19.

10. "Memorandoms—March 21ˢᵗ. [1763]," Founders Online, National Archives, https://founders.archives.gov/documents/Washington/01-01-02-0008-0010. Original source: *The Diaries of George Washington*, vol. 1, *11 March 1748–13 November 1765*, ed. Donald Jackson (Charlottesville: University Press of Virginia, 1976), 315–18.

11. General Ledger A, 1750–1772, Library of Congress, George Washington Papers, Series 5, Financial Papers.

12. "[Diary Entry: 11 October 1768]," Founders Online, National Archives, https://founders.archives.gov/documents/Washington/01-02-02-0003-0030-0005. Original source: *The Diaries of George Washington*, vol. 2, *14 January 1766–31 December 1770*, ed. Donald Jackson (Charlottesville: University Press of Virginia, 1976), 106.

13. George Mason, Letter to George Washington, April 5, 1785, accessed at the Constitutional Sources Project, https://www.consource.org/document/george-mason-to-george-washington-1785-4-5/20130122082428.

14. "Virginia Nonimportation Resolutions, 22 June 1770," Founders Online, National Archives, https://founders.archives.gov/documents/Jefferson/01-01-02-0032. Original source: *The Papers of Thomas Jefferson*, vol. 1, *1760–1776*, ed. Julian P. Boyd (Princeton, NJ: Princeton University Press, 1950), 43–48.

15. "Thomas Jefferson to James Mease, 29 June 1814," Founders Online, National Archives, https://founders.archives.gov/documents/Jefferson/03-07-02-0331. Original source: *The Papers of Thomas Jefferson*, Retirement Series, vol. 7, *28 November 1813 to 30 September 1814*, ed. J. Jefferson Looney (Princeton, NJ: Princeton University Press, 2010), 444–45.

16. "From Thomas Jefferson to Ellen Wayles Randolph Coolidge, 19 March 1826," Founders Online, National Archives, https://founders.archives.gov/documents/Jefferson/98-01-02-5969.

17. Thomas Jefferson, Farm Book, 1774–1824, 96, accessed at Thomas Jefferson Papers: An Electronic Archive, Massachusetts Historical Society, https://www.masshist.org/thomasjeffersonpapers/farm.

18. "From Thomas Jefferson to Thomas Mann Randolph, 4 February 1800," Founders Online, National Archives, https://founders.archives.gov/documents/Jefferson/01-31-02-0304. Original source: *The Papers of Thomas Jefferson*, vol. 31, *1 February 1799–31 May 1800*, ed. Barbara B. Oberg (Princeton, NJ: Princeton University Press, 2004), 359–61.

19. "Thomas Jefferson to Edmund Bacon, [15 November 1817]," Founders Online, National Archives, https://founders.archives.gov/documents/Jefferson/03-12-02-0153. Original source: *The Papers of Thomas Jefferson*, Retirement Series, vol. 12, *1 September 1817 to 21 April 1818*, ed. J. Jefferson Looney (Princeton, NJ: Princeton University Press, 2014): 192.

20. Robert Kenzer and *Dictionary of Virginia Biography*, "William Colson (1805–1835)." *Encyclopedia Virginia*, December 7, 2020, https://encyclopediavirginia.org/entries/colson-william-1805-1835.

21. Mary Newton Stanard, *Colonial Virginia, Its People and Customs* (Philadelphia, J.B. Lippincott, 1917), 128, accessed at https://www.google.com/books/edition/Colonial_Virginia/jx0SAAAAYAAJ.

22. *Lynchburg Virginian*, August 30, 1830, https://virginiachronicle.com/?a=d&d=LV18300830.

23. Ibid.

24. Ibid.

25. *Richmond Whig and Commercial Journal*, January 9, 1832, https://virginiachronicle.com/?a=d&d=RWCJ18320109.

26. Samuel Phillips Day, *Down South*, vol. 1 (Boston: n.p., 1860), 139.

27. Patricia Keppel Anderson and Monica Mitchell, "The Story Behind the Craft: Discovering Virginia's Beer History," https://www.virginia.org/blog/post/virginias-beer-history.

28. Oscar Edward Anderson, *Refrigeration in America: A History of a New Technology and Its Impact* (Princeton, NJ: Princeton University Press, 1953), 25.

29. "Davis, William," Encyclopedia of Detroit, Detroit Historical Society, https://detroithistorical.org/learn/encyclopedia-of-detroit/davis-william.

30. *Southern Planter*, November 1, 1857, https://virginiachronicle.com/?a=d&d=SPT18571101.

31. Homer Newton Frazier, interviewed by Dorothy Noble Smith, October 14, 1977, SdArch SNP-51, Shenandoah National Park Oral History Collection, 1964–99, Special Collections, Carrier Library, James Madison University, accessed at https://commons.lib.jmu.edu/cgi/viewcontent.cgi?article=1042&context=snp.

32. Cleadus A. Meadows, interviewed by Donna Noble Smith, June 11, 1979, SdArch SNP-90, Shenandoah National Park Oral History Collection, 1964–99, Special Collections, Carrier Library, James Madison University, accessed at https://commons.lib.jmu.edu/cgi/viewcontent.cgi?article=1075&context=snp.

33. Zada Lam, interviewed by Dorothy Noble Smith, August 3, 1978, SdArch SNP-79, Shenandoah National Park Oral History Collection,

1964–99, Special Collections, Carrier Library, James Madison University, accessed at https://commons.lib.jmu.edu/cgi/viewcontent.cgi?article=1069&context=snp.

34. Luther and Myra Wood, interviewed by Dorothy Noble Smith, October 15, 1979, SdArch SNP-134, Shenandoah National Park Oral History Collection, 1964–99, Special Collections, Carrier Library, James Madison University, accessed at https://commons.lib.jmu.edu/cgi/viewcontent.cgi?article=1112&context=snp.

35. Alistair Reece, "These Roots Grow Deep," *Pellicle*, June 16, 2021, https://www.pelliclemag.com/home/2021/6/14/these-roots-grow-deep-albemarle-ciderworks-north-garden-virginia.

36. Diane Flynt, *Wild, Tamed, Lost, Revived: The Surprising Story of Apples in the South* (Chapel Hill: University of North Carolina Press, 2023), 18.

37. Ibid., 33.

38. Tom Oliver, interview conducted by Alistair Reece, March 25, 2021.

Chapter 2

39. Reece, "These Roots Grow Deep."

40. Ibid.

41. Kirk Billingsley, interview conducted by Alistair Reece, January 31, 2024.

42. Ibid.

43. Mackenzie Smith, interview conducted by Alistair Reece, January 25, 2024.

44. Ibid.

45. Taylor Benson, interview conducted by Alistair Reece, January 25, 2024.

46. Ibid.

47. Jerry Thornton, interview conducted by Alistair Reece, April 18, 2024.

48. "The Drinker's Dictionary, 13 January 1737," Founders Online, National Archives, https://founders.archives.gov/documents/Franklin/01-02-02-0029. Original source: *The Papers of Benjamin Franklin*, vol. 2, *January 1, 1735, through December 31, 1744*, ed. Leonard W. Labaree (New Haven, CT: Yale University Press, 1961), 173–78.

49. Allen Crump, interview conducted by Alistair Reece, January 24, 2024.

50. Ibid.

51. Ibid.

52. Rob Campbell, interview conducted by Alistair Reece, February 7, 2024.

53. T. Glonti, "Traditional Technologies and History of Georgian Wine," *Le Bulletin de l'Organisation internationale de la vigne et du vin* (July–September 2010).

54. Lori Corcoran, interview conducted by Alistair Reece, January 31, 2024.

55. Ibid.

56. Ibid.

57. Eric Coiffi, interview conducted by Alistair Reece, March 6, 2024.

58. Ibid.

59. Ibid.

60. Ibid.

61. Jocelyn Kuzelka, interview conducted by Alistair Reece, April 19, 2024.

62. Larry Krietemeyer, interview conducted by Alistair Reece, February 2, 2024.

63. Ibid.

64. Ibid.

65. Scott Spelbring, interview conducted by Alistair Reece, January 26, 2024.

66. Ibid.

67. Ibid.

68. Ibid.

69. Tristan W. Wright, "2023, A Letter—Past, Present, and Future," Lost Boy Cider, 2023, https://www.lostboycider.com/2023-a-letter-past-present-and-future.

70. Stefanie Gans, "Bites: Mt Defiance Opens Its Cider Barn on Saturday," *Northern Virginia Magazine*, October 6, 2017, https://northernvirginiamag.com/food/food-news/2017/10/06/bites-mt-defiance-opens-its-cider-barn-on-saturday.

71. "Old Hill Cider Documentary," OldHillCider, November 21, 2013, YouTube video, https://www.youtube.com/watch?v=L4NpT_vWPSM.

72. Old Town Cidery, "About," https://www.oldtowncidery.com/about.

73. David Glaize, interview conducted by Alistair Reece, April 25, 2024.

74. Ibid.

75. Patrick Collins, interview conducted by Alistair Reece, January 27, 2024.

76. Zach Carlson, interview conducted by Alistair Reece, April 10, 2024.

77. Ibid.

78. Ibid.

79. Ibid.

80. Ibid.

81. Doug Smith, interview conducted by Alistair Reece, January 30, 2024.
82. Ibid.
83. Ibid.
84. Ibid.
85. Will Hodges, interview conducted by Alistair Reece, September 16, 2023.
86. Troddenvale at Oakley Farm, "Our Story," https://www.troddenvale.com/our-story.
87. Will Hodges, e-mail interview conducted by Alistair Reece, April 12, 2024.
88. Hodges, interview.
89. Troddenvale at Oakley Farm, "Visit Us." https://www.troddenvale.com/visit-us.
90. Justen Kelly Dick, interview conducted by Alistair Reece, September 15, 2023.
91. Ibid.
92. Ibid.
93. Mark Muse, interview conducted by Alistair Reece, December 10, 2023.
94. Mark Muse, interview conducted by Alistair Reece, January 20, 2024.
95. Ibid.
96. Stephen Schuurman, interview conducted by Alistair Reece, January 31, 2024.
97. Ibid.
98. Ibid.
99. Ibid.

Chapter 3

100. Diane Flynt, interview conducted by Alistair Reece, February 2, 2024.
101. K. Billingsley, interview conducted by Alistair Reece, September 16, 2023.
102. Vincent P. Magnini, *The Economic and Fiscal Impacts of Agritourism in Virginia* (Virginia Tech Pamplin College of Business, April 2017), https://www.vatc.org/wp-content/uploads/2020/01/The-Economic-and-Fiscal-Impacts-of-Agritourism-In-Virginia.pdf.
103. Flynt, *Wild, Tamed, Lost, Revived*, 13.
104. Diane Flynt, interview conducted by Alistair Reece, February 7, 2024.
105. Jocelyn Kuzelka, interview conducted by Alistair Reece, April 19, 2024.

106. Will Hodges, e-mail interview conducted by Alistair Reece, April 12, 2024.
107. David Glaize, interview conducted by Alistair Reece, April 25, 2024.
108. Ibid.
109. Code of Virginia, Title 4.1, Chapter 2 § 4.1-213. Manufacture and sale of cider, accessed from https://law.lis.virginia.gov/vacode/title4.1/chapter2/section4.1-213.
110. Scott Spelbring, e-mail interview, April 11, 2024.
111. Ibid.
112. David Glaize, interview conducted by Alistair Reece, April 25, 2024.
113. Spelbring, e-mail interview.
114. Chuck Shelton, e-mail interview conducted by Alistair Reece, April 20, 2024.
115. Allen Crump, e-mail interview conducted by Alistair Reece, April 10, 2024.
116. Mark Muse, e-mail interview conducted by Alistair Reece, April 10, 2024.
117. Patrick Collins, e-mail interview conducted by Alistair Reece, April 10, 2024.
118. Flynt, *Wild, Tamed, Lost, Revived*, 64.
119. Virginia Department of Energy, "Geology Mineral Resources," https://energy.virginia.gov/webmaps/GeologyMineralResources.
120. Lawrence D. Meinert, "The Science of Terroir," *Elements* 14, no. 3 (2018): 153–58, https://doi.org/10.2138/gselements.14.3.153.
121. Will Hodges, e-mail interview conducted by Alistair Reece, April 11, 2024.
122. Doug Smith, e-mail interview conducted by Alistair Reece, April 11, 2024.

INDEX

U

urbanization 28, 31, 32

V

Virginia Hewes Crab apple 18, 23,
     24, 32, 34, 36, 39, 44, 49, 53,
     55, 57, 66, 70, 80, 81, 89, 92,
     97, 99, 109, 114, 116, 118,
     119, 122, 124, 125, 128, 129,
     130, 136

W

Walker, Thomas 23, 40, 66
Washington, George 22, 23, 26, 40
Widow's Watch Cider 108, 109, 110
Wild Hare Cider 110, 111
Winchester Ciderworks 111, 112,
     113, 119

ABOUT THE AUTHORS

When not wrangling his twin sons, Alistair writes mostly about drinking and home brewing at Fuggled.net. An avid food tinkerer, he also loves to bake, make charcuterie, forage for fruit and find creative uses for the produce of his garden. Originally from the Highlands of Scotland, he now lives in rural Virginia, where he is developing worryingly strident opinions about barbecue.

When Mark started shooting freelance photography in 1999, he was using a Nikon FM2—a fully manual film camera. Shooting film forced him to concentrate on making a good exposure and on composing "in-camera," so that when he went into his tiny darkroom, he could emerge with hand-printed photographic art. Although he long ago moved to digital, Mark brings the same concentration on light, exposure and composition to the work he does today. More of Mark's work is available at blackgeckophotography.com.